J. Michael Cruz

Sociological Analysis of Aging
The Gay Male Perspective

"This is an important report on the well-being of gay middle-class men older than 55 and living in four Texas cities. Based on both survey and qualitative data, Cruz finds that these men enjoy long-term committed relationships and enduring networks of caring friends. Religion and spirituality play important roles in the lives of these men who primarily own their own homes outside a gay ghetto and report little interest in gay congregate housing. Most of the men report they are in good health, although a number of them report somewhat lowered morale.

Cruz supports his study with a careful and nuanced discussion of the literature on well-being and social needs of older gay men. His findings contradict assumptions that older gay men might have particular needs apart from other groups of older adults. They seek only the services which older adults generally enjoy in contemporary society. The men in this study were concerned only about being isolated as a group with particular needs or subject to stigma. This study is important reading for both those concerned with social policy and others studying sexuality and the life-course."

Bertram J. Cohler, PhD
William Rainey Harper Professor,
The Committee on Human Development
and the Departments of Psychology,
The University of Chicago

HPP

Harrington Park Press®
An Imprint of The Haworth Press, Inc.
New York • London • Oxford

Sociological Analysis of Aging
of Aging
The Gay Male Perspective

Sociological Analysis
of Aging
The Gay Male Perspective

J. Michael Cruz

HPP

Harrington Park Press®
An Imprint of The Haworth Press, Inc.
New York • London • Oxford

Published by

Harrington Park Press®, an imprint of The Haworth Press, Inc., 10 Alice Street, Binghamton, NY 13904-1580.

PUBLISHER'S NOTE
Identities and circumstances of individuals discussed in this book have been changed to protect confidentiality.

Cover design by Lora Wiggins.

Library of Congress Cataloging-in-Publication Data

Cruz, J. Michael.
    Sociological analysis of aging : the gay male perspective / J. Michael Cruz.
        p. cm.
Includes bibliographical references (p.   ) and index.
    ISBN 1-56023-453-9 (hard)—ISBN 1-56023-454-7 (soft)
    1. Aged gay men—Social conditions. 2. Aged gay men—Texas—Social conditions. I. Title.
    HQ76.14.C78 2003
    305.26—dc21
                                                                                        2003001804

For Minerva

ABOUT THE AUTHOR

J. Michael Cruz, PhD, is a native Texan now living in Maine. His training in sociology has equipped him to study inequality and the social injustices experienced by persons based on gender, race/ethnicity, social class, age, and sexual orientation. Within this framework, Dr. Cruz studies three specific research areas: aging gay men, gay male domestic violence, and HIV/AIDS.

CONTENTS

Foreword

Gerontology as a field has been slower to recognize cultural diversity and to welcome the fresh perspectives made possible by this recognition than disciplines such as sociology and women's studies have been. Only in the 1990s did a body of work finally challenge the white, middle-class, heterosexual, male paradigms of aging.

Aging research focusing on gay men, lesbians, bisexuals, and transgendered people is part of a larger effort to expand the vision of gerontology beyond the old models through cultural analysis, interdisciplinary work, and a keener awareness of the impact of ethnicity, gender, class, and sexual orientation.

In its contribution to the moral and scholarly work of making gay people more visible, *Sociological Analysis of Aging: The Gay Male Perspective* is thus a timely book, one that effectively refutes stereotyped notions of old gay men.

Although a few books and numerous articles have focused on aging as experienced by lesbians, gay men, bisexuals, and transgendered people, knowledge of aging in this community is fairly limited. Because the early work, valuable as it was, did not rest on much data, quantitative studies of gay aging are especially valuable.

J. Michael Cruz combines quantitative and qualitative research in his study of older gay men in four large cities in Texas. These men share some concerns with their heterosexual counterparts, but others are very specific to them. Cruz shows, for example, that the men have various strategies for coping with homophobia. Clearly, their aging has been shaped by their middle-class status, as well as by their sexual orientation.

Sociological Analysis of Aging demonstrates the importance of social networks for healthy aging among gay men. The voices of the author's subjects and his own interpretation of these voices advance our understanding of gay male lives. The book suggests possibilities for future research, for example, the impact of location on the aging of older gay men or the late-life social interactions of lesbians and gay men. The intersection of two stigmatized groups, homosexuals and older Americans, creates a number of issues worth exploring.

Margaret Cruikshank
Center on Aging
University of Maine

Preface

Elinor Johansen, professor extraordinaire, one day in a survey research methods class I was taking, said that sociologists study themselves. Although I do not intend to presume that all of us do this, I would be remiss in not explaining that my study on aging gay men is certainly an exploration of how I might navigate my own aging process.

The idea to study aging gay men came from taking courses at the University of North Texas for completion of the Specialist Certificate in Aging. Every one of these courses started in the same way. On the first day of class, professors inevitably would ask what the life stages in the aging process are (students would reply: "childhood, adolescence, adulthood," etc.) and follow up with questions about the experiences we go through as we age (e.g., dating, college, marriage, family, etc.). Time after time, in each class, I thought about how my life was different from the information provided.

Through these academic experiences, I came to recognize two important things. First, I realized that my life was qualitatively different, as are the lives of my gay friends. I also came to realize that the life trajectories of my heterosexual friends who are not interested in marrying are nonnormative. It was at this time that I realized how strongly we are socialized into thinking about marriage as a "natural" outcropping of the aging process. It is presumed that most individuals will eventually couple in the legal sense of the term. Those persons who cannot legally marry or refuse to do so are not only outside of our collective social imaginations but also generally left out of aging-related academic research and writing.

During my course work, professors were generally good about acknowledging an entire "other" population; however, no one seemed to know very much about aging gays. My class work revealed that very little has been written about aging gays. Within this "dearth in the literature" framework, I became concerned with two major issues: (1) the general reality is that we are living longer lives so that the population of aging persons is increasing, and (2) I was interested in finding out what life is like for aging gay men. Within this context I am and was curious about what the aging process will be like for the population of gays that is coming out at an earlier age and not necessarily living heterosexual lives before embarking on being openly homosexual. I also wonder how life will change as more of us age, and do so as openly gay men and lesbian women. I am interested in what sorts of legislative and social progress we will make as a nation regarding gays and lesbians. Last, I became curious about the role of Stonewall, the role of HIV/AIDS, and the importance of public figures being out—such as Ellen DeGeneres and Melissa Etheridge—and the impact these social realities have for the gay population, in general, and aging gays, specifically.

This book represents my interpretation of data collected from a specific population of aging gay men. I accept full responsibility for any errors, misrepresentations, or ambiguities. I also acknowledge that particular findings will be expounded upon in future research endeavors and that certainly this is only a small step in what I expect will become a more widely studied field. For instance, I was interested in the concept of disengaging. I wondered if aging gay men go through this process. I was also interested in the financial realities of aging gay men. Gays are not able to collect spousal Social Security or other forms of survivorship benefits. Moreover, some families often sue for monies left to the partner of a deceased gay family member.

With this in mind, I set out to explore the life situations of men in a particular age group. Ideally, I would have chosen the age of 65 and over, as men who are 55 to 65 presumably are more actively engaged in the labor force; however, I was concerned with not being able to find a large enough sample of gay men over 65 in Texas. With regard to social situations, I was interested in exploring the idea of disengagement. However, I was not able to study this because my sampling methodology entailed accessing only men who were socially engaged in one way or another. So, although I was able to study various levels of social engagement and involvement, I was not able to explore whether gay men became disengaged as they age because of this methodological bias.

I was also interested in housing. There is much rhetoric generated in gay-related magazines and newspapers about the need for gay-specific housing. I wanted to find out whether men in my study would in fact (1) assert the need and (2) indicate a desire to live in such a setting. I was surprised to find that although men did indicate the need, they said two things that I found surprising: (1) They did not want to live in gay-specific housing (or any sort of retirement or assisted-living housing); generally, men wanted to live in housing of their own choosing, and this meant staying in their own homes, and (2) Some people said that there was no need for gay-specific housing because they thought that in a few years gay and straight elderly would live together in the same sort of assisted-living or nursing facilities.

Financial realities was a topic I wanted to explore. I had countless talks during the interview process with respondents about the importance of compound interest. Frequently men would take on a paternal tone and look me right in the eye and ask, "Michael, are you saving for your future?" Quite frankly, I did not have the nerve to say that as a graduate student I was living hand to mouth, and the only thing I could think of was how much my cassette tapes and AA batteries were costing me to collect these interview data. I think for many of us retirement seems quite far off and not necessarily an immediate concern. This topic also was not as fleshed out as I would have liked. I tried to assess financial situations by asking about such things as educational attainment and employment and income status. I did not allow for having respondents who had retired and were reemployed to indicate that.

This study is the first in what I plan to be the major focus of my professional and research agenda. I aim not only to meet with men in different geographic regions of the country but also to collect data from a more diverse group of men. I also will inform aging-related theory and sociopolitical policy along the way. The voices of gay men (and lesbians, bisexuals, and other "queer" persons) need to be heard so that aging becomes manageable. My goal as a sociologist who studies aging gay men is to study men in various geographic regions and then revisit those areas at five-year intervals to ascertain whether conditions are improving for these populations.

This book is definitely an academic book. I do not pretend that it will be useful and interesting to everyone. However, I do think that persons working with elderly populations will be enlightened after reading the book. In addition, professionals in sociology, anthropology, political science, social work, and other related disciplines will be interested in what aging gay men have to say about the life process. Also, for those who are members of this population, reading the book and learning how others manage getting older will be useful. With this in mind, I have included the standard and relevant chapters for an academic monograph.

As with any research project, this book is not without its shortcomings. Future research projects should alleviate some of these. This book is not generalizable to the larger population. As a social constructionist, it is vital to allow one to self-identify as gay/homosexual/bisexual rather than impose the label and then randomly sample from a more representative group. With this in mind, I argue that one can never truly achieve a representative sample of queer persons.

This study is also biased in various ways. As previously mentioned, there is a bias in having studied only men who are socially engaged. All of these men were either involved in a social organization for aging gay men, were members of a primarily gay/lesbian church congregation, or were a friend of someone who was active in either of these. It is difficult to find social groups for aging gay men in particular regions of the country; however, it is even more difficult to know how to contact and include persons who fit criteria yet are not socially engaged. The other two biases reflect the composition of the social organizations used for entrée. Social-class bias and race bias exist. The majority of these men were educated and middle class. In addition, the number of men of color in this study is only 8 percent. The ultimate bias lies in my interpretation. My framework is that of social inequality so that I approach the topic of aging gay men from the perspective of social injustice. Quantitatively, the data speak for themselves; however, interpreting qualitative information is done from a social-conflict perspective.

I begin the book by placing the content in the perspective that there is not nearly enough information empirically documenting the life situations of aging gays and lesbians (and "queers") in general, and not enough information related to aging gay men specifically. This project is the first step in an attempt to fill some of that void. It is my intention to begin to shed light on a population that is very much a part of our society. In addition, this population is one that will need to be reckoned with, as we realize that current policies regarding such things as, for example, survivorship benefits and legally recognizing same-sex unions will begin to be more of an issue in the very near future. The numbers are increasing. Dare I say, "We're here. We're queer. Get used to it!"?

Acknowledgments

The 125 men who took part in this study especially need to be thanked and acknowledged for their input. This research project could not have been completed without their help. I would also like to thank Prime Timers Worldwide and the Metropolitan Community Church, Cathedral of Hope in Dallas, and Freedom Oaks in Austin, Texas, for allowing me to come to their facilities and collect data. My wonderful readers and mentors during the writing of this book Joyce Williams, Linda Marshall, Lisa Garza, Jeff Huber, and Keith Turner. Special thanks to Joyce Williams for her constant advice, positive criticisms, and quick turnaround.

I must thank and acknowledge my family and friends for their constant encouragement throughout the years and the writing process. My family members were wonderful. I appreciate the support. Marco, Rob, and Minerva are invaluable. I cannot say enough about their unconditional love and the manner in which they have kept me grounded for many, many years.

Chapter 1

Introduction

The process of aging is one that everyone experiences. Persons of different races and ethnicities, those of religious or spiritual beliefs, men and women, and heterosexuals and homosexuals all go through the aging process. However, there is a gap in the social science literature when it comes to the topic of aging homosexuals. The gerontological literature is typically heterosexist and describes aging in ways that may be foreign to persons who are not heterosexual (see Papalia et al. 1996; Atchley 2000). Little empirical data exist on persons who are homosexual, and even less data exist on homosexual individuals who are aging. However, as far back as the Kinsey Report in the 1950s, it has been estimated that, minimally, 8 to 10 percent of the U.S. population is homosexual (see Kimmel 1978; Berger 1982). Recently, the 2000 U.S. Census documented the number of unmarried couples who cohabitated. This number was 3.8 million households or 3.7 percent of the total households (Fields and Casper 2001). Certainly one may argue several things: (1) Heterosexual persons are included in this category; (2) not all same-sex couples live together; and (3) Many gays/lesbians are not partnered. All of these are true; however, we are finally getting data on gay/lesbian couple households. Furthermore, not only have more recent researchers looked at the gay population in particular (Black et al. 2000), but the aging gay population has also begun to be examined at a social policy level (Cahill et al. 2000). With the assumption that homosexual persons may experience the aging process in ways that differ from those described in the gerontological literature, this research proposed to describe perceptions about aging as reported by older gay men.

PURPOSE

The purpose of this study was to examine the life situations of some aging gay men who are Texas residents. The objectives were to gain an understanding of the actual life changes these men experience as homosexuals as they age and to describe their physical, mental, and social needs. Original research was conducted and findings compared with the existing literature on this population.

RESEARCH PROBLEM

This research represents an attempt to contribute to the literature related to a population that is substantial and influential yet under-studied. A select group of aging homosexual males was studied by examining a general research question: How do gay males approach and experience aging? A survey instrument was used to gather data related to aging homosexual men in the Texas cities of Austin, Dallas, Houston, and San Antonio. Participants were asked to provide demographic data as well as answer questions relevant to the aging experience of gay men in Texas. The areas examined were health and well-being, interpersonal relationships/involvements and the availability of a social support system, experiences with employment and retirement, and presumed current and future housing needs. In addition to the survey conducted in four cities, in-depth qualitative interviews were used to examine the life situations and aging experiences of gay males who live in the geographic area of Dallas, Texas.

RATIONALE

Information related to the aging process is largely heterosexist. Representative of this literature, for example, is Papalia et al. (1996) and Atchley (2000) who documented major developments in three periods of adulthood (i.e., young adulthood, middle age, and late adulthood) and ascertained the impact of events such as child rearing, empty-nest syndrome, and grandparenting. No mention is made of persons who, because of their sexual orientation, may not go through these stages or may experience alternative processes specific to their sexual orientation. Although Atchley (2000) does address diversity in aging, the concept of diversity is utilized to include differences related to social class, race/ethnicity, and culture. Much of the existing literature on aging gay men is dated, inconclusive, and based on case studies or limited samples. For example, a study conducted by Berger (1982) in 1978 presents aging gay men as a happy and well-adjusted sexual minority.* Is Berger's work representative of other gay men? Do his findings hold more than twenty years later? Were his findings specific to a population of men within a certain geographic region?

Knowing more about all segments of the aging population as well as understanding something of what can be done to assist in "successful" aging for sexual minorities will enhance the quality of life for persons within this population. Research related to aging gay men is vital, especially as the elderly begin to constitute a larger proportion of the U.S. population. In 1999 there were 24.7 million men in the United States aged 55 and older (Smith and Tillipman 2000). Meyer (2000) indicates that the 2000 U.S. Census documented 35 million or 12 percent of our nation's population was 65 or older. Moreover, the age group with the largest percentage growth was persons aged 50 to 54. The age group of 55 and older is expected to reach 46,994,000 by the year 2025 (U.S. Census Bureau (2000). As it relates specifically to Texas, the U.S. Census indicates the numbers of men aged 65 and older will jump to 1,327,000 by 2005, 1,734,000 by 2015, and 2,393,000 by the year 2025 (U.S. Census Bureau, 2003). Although there are no estimates as to the number of persons in Texas who are homosexual, as with the nation, it may be assumed that an estimated 8 to 10 percent of the popula-

---

*Berger's work included men as young as forty.

tion is homosexual, although they may not self-identify or openly identify as such (see Kimmel 1978; Berger 1982).

RESEARCH QUESTIONS

The guiding research questions for this study are as follows:

1. What are the housing needs of the aging gay male community?
   - What housing needs are anticipated in the future?
2. How do aging gay men describe their health and well-being?
   - Do aging gay men consider themselves to be physically healthy?
   - Do members of this population perceive themselves as suffering from depression?
   - If they do consider themselves to be depressed, what do they perceive as the cause?
3. Do members of this group have access to social support networks?
4. How involved are aging gay men with family, friends, church, and community?

GEOGRAPHIC SETTINGS

This research project was carried out in Austin, Dallas, Houston, and San Antonio, Texas. These are four of the largest cities in the state with, presumably, the most available research participants. Dallas and Houston are the largest cities, with San Antonio coming in third, and Austin fourth. These locations were chosen because each has a chapter of the Prime Timers, a worldwide organization for mature gay and bisexual men. It was anticipated that active chapters of this organization would provide a potential pool of persons in the needed age and sexual orientation categories to participate in this project.

Although the men studied are not presumed to be representative of their cities, differences in the cities and in how they contextualize their gay communities may, in fact, predetermine certain differences among participants. Austin occupies 272.19 square miles and had a population of 656,562 in 2000. The city's Web site indicates "Austin is now the fourth largest city in the state and the sixteenth most populous city in the nation" (Austin City Connection 2003). This city lacks a specific geographic region where primarily gay and lesbian persons live. Although no numbers can be given for the city's gay population, an Internet search provided information on the Austin Gay and Lesbian Chamber of Commerce and various other social and political organizations in the city for persons who are homosexual. In addition, Austin does not have a gay/lesbian yellow pages, but gay community newspapers (where businesses catering to the gay communities in various Texas cities are listed) list various businesses or agencies specific to the Austin area.

Dallas occupies 378.4 square miles and its 2000 population was listed as 1,188,580, with a median age in the range of 25 to 34 (Dallas Facts and Statistical Profile 2003). With regard to opportunities for homosexuals in the city, Dallas has the Resource Center of Dallas that lists contact information for many gay social and political organizations in the area, such as the Metropolitan Community Church. In addition, this city has a gay/lesbian yellow pages, which is a telephone directory comprising gay-owned/operated or gay-friendly businesses in the Dallas area. Dallas also has a gay community and an area of town with some gay-owned businesses.

"Houston is the fourth most populous city in the nation" boasts the city's Web site. The 2000 population of Houston was 1.9 million people (City of Houston 2003). This city boasts the Greater Houston Gay and Lesbian Chamber of Commerce, a gay/lesbian community center, a gay/lesbian yellow pages, and a large geographic area known as "the gay community."

"San Antonio, the third-largest city in Texas and the seat of Bexar county, is located in the south-central part of the state, on the San Antonio River" (San Antonio, Texas 2003). The city occupies 408 square miles; the 2000 population was 1,144,646; and the median age was 31.7 (San Antonio, Texas 2003). An Internet search revealed a Gay San Antonio Web site that reported its mission is to "bring together harmony, understanding, and diversity . . . [and enable] thought, reflection, and personal growth" (Gay San Antonio 2001). San Antonio also lacks a structured geographic region where the majority of residents are homosexual; however, the gay community newspapers list businesses (nightclubs, gay-friendly restaurants, etc.) in the area.

FOCUS OF THIS RESEARCH

The substantitive areas addressed within this project included social support and involvement, housing, health and well-being, and employment status. In addition, some concluding questions included asking the respondents to reflect on their lives. Thus, persons were asked what, if anything, was left on a "to-do" list; what the best aspects of aging are; what the worst aspects of aging are; and what, if anything, they would change about the way their lives have gone. These issues are expounded upon as follows.

Social Support/Involvement

This aspect of the research is designed to describe the self-reported social support systems and social involvements of aging gay males. Some stereotypes depict the population as solitary and lonely individuals, and others describe healthy, involved aging gay men (Berger 1996). All respondents in the Berger study had the social support of gay male friends. Many had the support of peers and were able to relate to other gay men who were of the same age group. All men in the study participated regularly in one or more gay community institutions (gay churches, social service organizations, or gay rights groups), so that, again, participants were engaged not only in the gay community but also in the aging gay male community. Berger (1984) also called for social support services specific to the homosexual community and he implored social workers to become aware of the realities of homosexual aging. Berger asserts, "integration into a homosexual community is an important factor in the adaptation of older male homosexuals" (1996, p. 38).

Furthermore, he indicates, "contact with other gays is so important to older gay men's adjustment" (Berger 1996, p. 40). Also related to family and social support, Lipman (1986, p. 54) found that the importance of one's intimate, same-sex relationships could be paralleled to the importance of a heterosexual's relationship with a spouse. An issue with the aging gay population is also the reality of caregiving and social support needs that are particular to aging gays. Fredriksen (1999) addressed the caregiving responsibilities of gays and lesbians and found that gays who care for aging parents/adults or children have needs that are specific to their community.

Housing

Housing is a concern for most persons as they age. The primary concerns often focus on whether an individual will be able to care for himself or herself or have a companion. Whether persons can stay in their own homes or will require assisted living or total care are other concerns. Very little information regarding housing for homosexuals exists, and only one study has been found specific to elderly homosexuals. Page (1998) documented discriminatory practices of landlords dealing with openly gay persons trying to rent a place to live. Lucco (1987) conducted a survey in which gay and lesbian persons documented their desires for same-sex housing. Respondents were able to indicate specifically what they wanted in a planned retirement community.

There is currently no housing (either assisted-living or long-term care facilities) specifically for same-sex couples or for (single) homosexual men in the Dallas/Fort Worth area that is not AIDS specific. In fact, there seems to be no housing for this community within the state of Texas. Recently, however, information has been generated regarding the possibility of creating local gay/lesbian long-term housing facilities. In addition, mention has been made regarding a nonintensive care or independent living facility; thus, discussions about assisted living for aging gays are being generated (see Devlin 2000). Current gay-specific housing can be found in the San Francisco Bay Area. A facility known as Gaycare is a "residential care facility specializing in the care of gay males over sixty, and those under sixty with like needs" ("An Introduction to Gaycare" 2001, p. 1).

Health and Well-Being

One's emotional well-being is paramount to maintaining a healthy mental and physical self. Such emotional well-being presumably increases one's ability to successfully navigate the aging process. Kimmel (1978) asserts that aging gays have particular needs, aside from those of aging persons in general (see also Adelman 1991; McDougall 1993). Berger (1984) asserts that homosexual persons are emotionally and mentally better off when they are able to associate with others like themselves, as opposed to when they are either isolated or only socializing with heterosexuals. The need for HIV/AIDS services (physical and mental-health related) impacts some aging gay men as well (Wallace et al. 1993). Anxiety over death was studied by Templer et al. (1983). It was found to be an issue important to the gay/lesbian community, perhaps because the usual forms of social support may not be available. Questions can also be raised about homophobia and whether it impacts the quality of life for aging gay males (Friend 1990; McDougall 1993).

With regard to physical health, the American Medical Association (AMA) documents the responsibilities of physicians with regard to meeting the special needs of the gay and lesbian community. Needs or concerns that are particular to gay men include HIV, hepatitis, cancer, and various sexually transmitted diseases. The AMA stresses the importance of physicians obtaining a sexual history since gay men do not usually divulge their sexual orientation to their doctors. By way of illustration, the authors assert that in a 1992 study "44 percent of . . . gay men . . . did not reveal their sexual orientation" nor did many respondents divulge their HIV-positive status to their physicians (AMA Council on Scientific Affairs 1996, p. 1356). This report asserts that when physicians fail to ask and respondents fail to volunteer the information, patients are assumed to be heterosexual. When this happens, the physician does not provide the best health care service that could be given, thus leaving the specific medical needs of patients in this situation unmet.

The Gay and Lesbian Medical Association (GLMA), in conjunction with the National Coalition for Lesbian/Gay/Bisexual/Transgendered Health, has written a 500-page document to accompany the recently released national public health agenda (Gay and Lesbian Medical Association and LGBT Health Experts 2001). The initiative of the Healthy People 2010 program "is a set of health objectives for the Nation to achieve over the first decade of the new century" (Gay and Lesbian Medical Association and LGBT Health Experts 2001). This companion document to the Healthy People 2010 agenda outlines the diversity of the community (Gay and Lesbian Medical Association and LGBT Health Experts 2001). This is the first time that gays and lesbians have been properly acknowledged in a national health initiative.

Employment

The employment status of persons within the gay aging population is of interest not only for demographic purposes but to provide descriptive information about the reality of issues related to retirement, remaining engaged, and financial stability. The gerontological literature treats retirement as a major life event for most, particularly males. Because males identify so closely with their occupations, retirement may not be a pleasant stage to approach or go through (see Papalia et al. 1996; Atchley 2000). In addition, men who were socialized in the 1940s and 1950s (as were the participants) frequently think of self-worth in terms of what they do/did for a living, and it is presumed that letting a career go will be equivalent to giving up a part of their lives (see Papalia et al. 1996; Atchley 2000). One of the practical reasons for the difficulty of retirement is that, suddenly, there are supposedly no demands, requirements, or schedule; there is no place to be at any particular time. This life change (one of presumed leisure) is often difficult to manage. The retired male may feel as though he is not needed. Last, the opportunity to remain employed has financial advantages. Retirement may mean reduced benefits and sometimes a very drastic life change with regard to finances and resulting opportunities to travel or spend leisure time.

SUMMARY

This chapter has presented a general overview of the research project, with demographic justifications for studying the aging population of gay males. Research questions have been posed and a brief literature review has been offered. In subsequent chapters, a theoretical base will be generated, the literature will be expounded upon, the research methods will be delineated, and the participants will be described. Findings will be organized and presented in relation to the research questions. Concluding remarks will include suggestions for social policy as well as for study in the area of gerontology, in general, with a more focused need for research related to aging homosexual persons.

Chapter 2

Literature Review

All mainstream gerontological literature has a heterosexist slant. More often than not, gays are excluded from relevant discussions (see Papalia et al. 1996; Atchley 2000). This forgotten population has not been studied in depth for various reasons, one of which is the group's relative invisibility. The social stigma associated with homosexuality means that some gay men, for instance, find it difficult to lead their lives as openly homosexual persons. In addition, issues related to self-identification may be another reason for a lack of research regarding this population. Whatever the reason, it has been estimated by a number of different sources that from 8 to 10 percent of the United States population as a whole is homosexual (see Kimmel 1978), and the needs of this segment of our population will eventually have to be addressed as our nation ages (see Kimmel 1978; Berger 1982). The U.S. Census has shown us that our population is aging, however, the government is finally beginning to document the "unmarried households" to indicate both unmarried heterosexuals who cohabitate and homosexuals who do this as well. Although the sexuality is not queried, and the numbers of single or noncohabitating gays/lesbians is lacking, these numbers are nevertheless important. It was the goal of this research to illuminate the life situations of aging gay men with regard to their health and well-being, their social support and interpersonal relationships, and their perceived housing needs. A search of the literature in each of these areas has revealed that little or no empirical work has been done specific to gay males.

Many negative stereotypes portray the aging gay man as a "tragic figure" (Berger 1996, p. 26). In fact, some of the beliefs are that as the homosexual male ages

> he becomes increasingly effeminate . . . he is alienated from friends and family . . . he lives alone, not by choice, but by necessity. Since he is no longer sexually attractive to other homosexuals, he is forced to prey on children and pursue anonymous sexual contacts in public places such as restrooms and parks. He is desperately unhappy. (Berger 1996, p. 25)

This negative stereotype has been documented by other researchers. For example, Dorfman et al. (1995) examined the assumption that older gays are, in fact, more depressed and socially isolated than older nongays, while Kelly (1977) investigated whether gays were oversexed (while experiencing an unsatisfactory sex life), isolated, closeted, and effeminate. Interestingly, Dorfman et al. (1995, p. 29) found that "there [were] no significant differences between older heterosexuals and older homosexuals in regard to depression and social support" and the only variation was that gays relied more on friends than family members for support, while the opposite was true for heterosexuals. Likewise, Kelly (1977, p. 331) found that "there seems to be no further rationale for the application of certain blanket stereotypes about aging gay men . . . as these assertions are not always accurate." Kelly suggests that although being gay does not seem to cause problems for aging persons, social stigma does cause problems for aging gays.

GAY AGING

Berger has been virtually the lone authority on aging gay males (1982, 1984, 1996). He has studied the realities of aging gays and has been able to discover and address some positive aspects of aging as a homosexual. Berger argues that these persons are less likely to experience role loss, perhaps as a result of not becoming involved in many roles (especially those that are family oriented, e.g., father, husband, etc.), and that in dealing with the stigma associated with being homosexual, they are often better prepared to deal with the stigma associated with aging (Berger 1982). Likewise, he asserts that the negative stereotypes of gay aged persons as being disengaged from heterosexuals and other homosexuals, or disinterested in forming families of their own, are not true. Berger not only asserts that negative stereotypes of aging gay men are untrue, he also found that gay men could actually have very positive or successful aging experiences. By way of illustration, when asked what makes a gay man adjust well to growing old, respondents indicated that awareness of one's "place" within the larger society and self-acceptance regarding one's homosexuality enables this adjustment (Berger 1984). Berger presented a prototype of the healthy aging gay male:

> Age was associated with a greater self-acceptance, fewer psychosomatic symptoms, and greater life satisfaction. The older homosexual male who is most likely to be psychologically well adjusted will be highly integrated into the homosexual community, unwilling to change his homosexuality, less concerned with concealment, perceiving his health as good or excellent, having a current exclusive relationship with another man, and reporting a high level of satisfaction with his sex life. (Berger 1984, p. 215)

According to Berger, the prevailing negative beliefs about aging gay men are untrue, and the reality is that if the gay male accepts his place within the larger society and accepts his homosexuality, he can perhaps have a very positive experience with the aging process. The problem is that very little empirical research exists to validate, refute, or extend Berger's work.

Friend (1990) has written a conceptual piece regarding a theoretical model for successful aging. He fits homosexuals into one of three typologies: stereotypic older lesbian/gay; passing older lesbian/gay; and affirmative older lesbian/gay. The process of aging, according to Friend (1990), is successful when persons challenge heterosexism and minimize homophobia. Adelman (1991) studied 27 gay men and 25 lesbians to examine the life situations of aging homosexuals and to address the realities of stigma and homophobia. She indicates that accepting one's gayness makes it easier to accept the aging process. This idea of challenging heterosexism and being out or openly gay as opposed to being closeted is also purported by Rosenfeld as being a positive or helpful part of aging. She examines cohort identities and indicates that

> [i]t is the elderly gay liberationists who are lionized by younger generations of homosexuals, portrayed in terms often used to construct war heroes, while the discreditable [i.e. persons who remain closeted or keep their homosexuality a secret] elderly are offered little, if any, political recognition. (Rosenfeld 1999, p. 139)

This same finding of self-acceptance as a homosexual (for the enabling of a positive or successful aging process) is also indicated in an earlier work by Minnigerode and Adelman (1978, p. 454) who state that "gaining self acceptance and self esteem were mentioned by almost every respondent" in their study.

HEALTH AND WELL-BEING

Mental/Psychological Health

In order for one to have a successful aging experience one needs to maintain a healthy mental and physical state. How that manifests itself for an individual is less important than having the experience be functional in that capacity. Kimmel (1978), through the use of qualitative data gathered from 14 gay men over the age of 55 in New York City, documents that aging gay men have needs that are particular to this community. Among the needs cited are support during bereavement, assistance for the physically disabled, and a reduction in stigmatization (see also Adelman 1991; McDougall 1993). Berger (1984) asserts that homosexuals are emotionally and mentally better off when they are able to associate with others like themselves, as opposed to when they are either isolated or socializing only with heterosexuals. HIV/AIDS may produce needs that impact some aging gay men as well (Wallace et al. 1993). Exemplifying the need for social support, Templer et al. (1983) found that usual forms of family support are sometimes not available to gays. His study focuses on anxiety experienced by aging gays—in particular that related to death and dying. Also related to the support needs of the gay community in general, several have documented the existence of homophobia and question whether it is an effect on the aging process for gays (Friend 1990; McDougall 1993).

Literature in the area of psychological therapy indicates that elderly persons who are homosexual do have specific needs and concerns that are frequently unlike those of heterosexual persons in the same age cohort. One concern of aging gay men is that of loss. Although loss in general is a part of growing old, and elderly people do experience various types of role loss, the support or lack of it available to gay, lesbian, bisexual, and transgender (GLBT) elderly makes the experience of loss different. Woodman (1989) studied 100 leaders in lesbian and gay campus organizations who attended a two-day conference. Participants in one group were asked to engage in discussions related to stresses experienced by lesbians and gay men. They were also asked to identify five stressful situations or problems which they believed were unique to lesbians and gay men. Woodman's findings indicate that gays experience several types of loss including self-esteem, spiritual supports, family, and job/income, and, in addition, anticipate loss of such things as identity and relationships (Woodman 1989, p. 54). McDougall (1993) indicates specific needs of the aging gay community (addressed in the existing literature) as individuals experience such things as anxiety bereavement, homophobia, and dissatisfaction with sexual identity and intimacy. Finally, Ross et al. (1988) report that the mental health needs of the gay community must be taken seriously while allowing for cross-cultural sensitivity so as not to ignore the needs of homosexual men who are dealing with issues not rooted in Western culture. With this in mind, the clinician or social service professional who works with an elderly gay population needs to be aware of differences and able to effectively address these special needs within a cross-cultural setting.

Carlson and Steuer (1985), using a sample of 549 heterosexual and homosexual men and women studied the aging process and its impact on mental health. Interestingly, a negative correlation was found with the homosexual men between age and depression scores, suggesting that as gay men age, they are less likely to suffer from depression. Kertzner (1999, p. 57), who studied gay men ages 41 to 55, found that aging "was not accompanied by reports of psychological distress or social disengagement in spite of assumptions to that effect." Kimmel (1978, p. 533) also found that "the stereotypes of the lonely, depressed, sexually frustrated aging gay man are not valid." He asserts that aging gays have specific advantages over heterosexual elderly because they experience a "continuity of life, conscious preparation for self-reliance during the later years, experience in all the relevant skills for maintaining oneself and one's home, and a self-created friendship network and social supports" (p. 524).

Slusher et al. (1996) have documented the importance of support groups for elderly persons by addressing the historical development of a social support group for elderly gay and lesbian people. Furthermore, they assert that research has tended to be over representative of "white, educated individuals connected to the gay community through organizations, bars, community centers, and churches" and that there is a need to understand persons which researchers are not able to meet (p. 121). This article describes a successful organization called Gays and Lesbians Older and Wiser (GLOW) that reaches those who are typically excluded from gay social life and

> provides a safe space for older gay men and lesbians in one local region to meet and identify one another and to engage in

mutual support in a non-gay-identified suburban community
setting. (Slusher et al. 1996, p. 118)

There is little doubt that social groups are important. However,
for persons who do not have access to a gay group or community
setting, Galassi (1991, p. 75) has developed a workshop in which
gays and lesbians can engage in a life-review process since "gay
and lesbian elders have not [necessarily] enjoyed the public, community organized recognition of significant life markers." Some of
the life markers that Galassi (1991) asserts gays and lesbians do
not experience include marriage and parenting. His support group
model utilizes five very structured sessions, which include discussion or exercises related to topics such as a gay health agenda, spirituality, and family. This therapeutic form of interaction is another
way for persons to come together and remain engaged both socially
and psychologically and, in so doing, embrace their homosexual
selves. In the absence of more structured support groups, such as
those addressed by Slusher et al. (1996), perhaps persons in social
service agencies will be able to utilize the more applied approach
posited by Galassi (1991).

In relation to psychological health and, again, negative stereotypes of elderly persons in general, and elderly homosexuals in
particular, Dorfman et al. (1995) studied 108 homosexual and heterosexual elderly men and women and found that 15 percent were
depressed. This rate is consistent with depression in the elderly
population in general (Dorfman et al. 1995). After the researchers
controlled for level of education, gender, and partner status, no
significant difference in depression was found between the heterosexual and homosexual groups. Kelly (1977, p. 330) found that the
gay men in his study "do not seem to fit the stereotypes which
mark them as lonely, sexually frustrated, and unhappy" although
he did find such things as stigma related to homosexuality among
the problems specific to aging gay men. The other major problems
specific to aging gays discovered by Kelly (1977) were bereavement and physical disability.

Physical Health

In order to meet the needs of the gay/lesbian community, the American Medical Association (AMA) formally specifies physician responsibilities for dealing with persons in this community. (AMA Council on Scientific Affairs 1996). For example, gay men may be at increased risk for such ailments as HIV, hepatitis, cancer, and various sexually transmitted diseases. It is critical that gay men receive particular treatments, such as a hepatitis B vaccine and colorectal cancer screenings. It is documented that physicians often do not ask patients their sexual orientation and that patients often do not divulge their sexual identity. When this lack of communication occurs, the result is inevitably a health care situation in which the needs of a gay/lesbian person cannot possibly be fully met. In fact, almost one-half of patients in one study did not tell physicians their sexual orientation. Furthermore, many did not communicate their HIV status to their health care providers (AMA Council on Scientific Affairs 1996). This lack of communication generally enables the physician to assume a patient is heterosexual and potentially not investigate, diagnose, and treat ailments that are more likely to impact the homosexual community. The report claims that "taking a sexual history in a nonjudgmental and attentive manner with open-ended questions can help the patient feel comfortable and willing to confide in the physician" (AMA Council on Scientific Affairs 1996, p. 1356). This nonjudgmental attitude reminds physicians that it is certain behaviors which put gay men at risk for particular ailments, rather than sexual orientation per se.

A major breakthrough as it relates to the physical health of gay and lesbian persons is the health initiative recently released by the federal government called Healthy People 2010 (Office of Disease Prevention and Health Promotion, U.S. Department of Health and Human Services 2001a). This is a national agenda with two main goals: (1) increase quality and years of healthy life and (2) eliminate health disparities. The initiative also addresses ten leading health indicators and several areas of focus. Among the leading health indicators are responsible sexual behavior and access to health care.

HIV is included in one of the focus areas. The GLMA has also released a document supporting this report, which indicates health care needs that are specific to the GLBT community. This is the first time in the history of the federal government that such a document has been offered in conjunction with the nation's ten-year health initiative plans. The document aims to educate the medical community (and the GLBT community) about issues specially related to the health maintenance of persons in this community. For example, the document asserts the importance of regular immunizations, in addition to being immunized for hepatitis A, hepatitis B, and influenza (Gay and Lesbian Medical Association and LGBT Health Experts 2001).

HIV/AIDS

It is important to deal with the issue of HIV/AIDS in any population, but it has a greater importance when addressing the communities of both gay men and the elderly. The Centers for Disease Control and Prevention (CDC) offer various statistics. As of December 2001, there were 184, 515 persons living with HIV infection in the United States. With regard to new HIV infections, 70 percent of those are occurring in men (Centers for Disease Control and Prevention 2001c). Futhermore, there were 344,178 living with AIDS (Centers for Disease Control and Prevention 2001b). The number of persons in the 55 and older age group living with AIDS is 47,733 (Centers for Disease Control and Prevention 2001a). In the state of Texas 10,646 persons are living with HIV and 24,936 are living with AIDS as of the end of 2001 (Centers for Disease Control and Prevention 2001b).

Moss and Miles (1987) conducted a study to examine HIV infection rates in an older population and found that 10 percent of AIDS cases have occurred in the age group of 50 years and older, with 25 percent occurring in the population aged 65 and older, and 4 percent in persons who are 70 years of age and older. Noting the more recent statistics reported by the CDC, Moss and Miles (1987) make an argument for the need to educate older populations about HIV transmission and safe-sex/intravenous (IV) drug use tactics.

In addition, several researchers have noted that the elderly are persons frequently left out of the HIV/AIDS prevention education agenda based on misconceptions regarding their lack of sexual activity or IV drug use (Emlet 1997). Such misconceptions regarding the aging population (and specifically the aging gay male population) are problematic because the result is that these persons are not being targeted with HIV prevention education, nor are they being tested for HIV/AIDS when they present themselves in a medical setting with symptoms. Emlet (1997) indicates that men having sex with men (among the population of persons aged 50 and over) still accounts for most AIDS cases (see also Scharnhorst 1992). Gordon and Thompson (1995) also indicate that 38 percent of respondents in their study contracted HIV via male-to-male sex. Finally, Wallace et al. state "homosexual or bisexual behavior remains the predominant risk factor for HIV infection up to age 70" (1993, p. 61). This information is important for the medical community (so that persons are targeted for HIV prevention education and/or tested for HIV when presenting themselves for medical attention); for the social service community (who presumably will counsel and deal with emotional/psychological needs of those impacted); and also for members of the community at large—gays, straights, HIV positive, and HIV negative. Kowalewski (1988) indicates that gay men are frequently ambivalent toward persons with AIDS so that although they cannot forget or overlook them, they fail to get involved in any real sense.

SOCIAL SUPPORT/RELATIONSHIPS/INVOLVEMENT

A small body of literature exists related to social support workers and therapists dealing with gays and/or elderly gays. The literature is quite positive for persons in the gay community, as it generally implores those working in a therapeutic relationship to be sensitive to the needs of homosexuals. Addressing the literature in an evolutionary manner, Fort et al. (1971, p. 348) studied 163 professional therapists who averaged about 5 percent of clients who were homosexual. Of particular interest in this study is that when asked about counseling a client with the goal of changing his or her sexual orientation, 38 percent said they would, while 43 percent said they would not. Thompson and Fishburn (1977, p. 129) reported that education is needed for graduate students in counselor training so that "the counselor trainee should be . . . comfortable enough with homosexuality to allow the client 'to be' homosexual." DeCrescenzo (1984) writes about the training of social service agents as well, and indicates that although students who are acquainted with a homosexual are less homophobic than others, there is still a need for training in the area of homosexuality in a manner that removes gays from a setting whereby homosexuality is discussed solely in a human sexuality program, rather than in a manner that addresses homosexuals as being a part of the larger society. According to DeCrescenzo, this type of training frames homosexuals in a clinical and aberrant manner. Furthermore, she asserts that a helpful training program would include "factual information; theoretical material; and participative experience" (DeCrescenzo 1984, p. 132). Finally, Gochros (1984, pp. 148-151) asserts that the academic training of social work students should include such things as conceptualization of community attitudes which have created sexual oppression; direct contact with homosexual persons; research; and the provision of medical, religious, and legal information related to homosexuality.

As it relates to social support and involvement Berger (1984) asserts the need for an aging gay male to occupy the same social space and time with others like him. He does this by documenting not only integration into an aging gay male community but also indicates that this sort of social contact is necessary for old-age adjustment. He queried respondents about their involvement with gay male friends, community organizations, and churches (Berger 1996, p. 40). All respondents in his study had the social support of gay male friends. Many had the support of peers so that respondents were able to relate to other gay men who were of the same age group. Men in the Berger (1996) study were, in fact, socially engaged in various gay-specific community organizations. Thus they were in touch with peer groups related to their sexual identity but also those in their specific age cohorts.

Berger (1996) interviewed aging gay men about involvement with family members and various patterns emerged. For instance, some respondents remained closeted and had not divulged their homosexuality to friends and family. In fact, one respondent is quoted as saying that his wife and children did not know that he was gay because he assumed they would not be able to handle the news. Another pattern was that many respondents had lost their parents before they were able to divulge their homosexuality. For persons whose sexuality was known to family members, responses ranged from supportive to not supportive. Lipman (1986) argues that the importance of a same sex relationship resembles that of a heterosexual relationship, so family and social support is vital.

Caregiving and social support needs in the gay community are important to address as well and Fredriksen (1999) has done some of this work. Some of the problems experienced by homosexuals with caregiving responsibilities include such things as custody battles for children or problems with school authorities. Those who are caring for an ill significant other may experience problems with medical personnel. Fredriksen calls for social support services that are responsive to this population.

HOUSING

Very little information regarding housing for homosexuals exists; however, there is a body of literature related to the elderly (not specific to heterosexuals, but presumably so) and housing. A portion of this literature relates specifically to the well-being of persons in long-term care facilities. For example, Black et al. (1997, p. 727) assert:

> Some residents who are at significantly higher risk of needing mental health care are also at significantly higher risk of not receiving it. These include males, those with no Medicare insurance, residents who are older, and those with more ADL [activities of daily living] impairments.

In another article, Black and associates (1999) report on placement in a long-term care facility and state that the "nursing home placement of elderly public housing residents is predicted primarily by functional status and mental status" (p. 565). Litwin (1998) examined social support and, specifically, reciprocal support in a long-term care facility and found that the types of informal support in this living facility were governed by the exchange ethic: residents helped one another with the hope or expectation of receiving aid in exchange at some future point in time. Last, related to housing quality and its availability, Markham and Gilderbloom (1998) document that region and race are most important in determining housing quality. They found that quality of housing is poorest for "blacks, in the South, for males living alone, and for renters" (Markham and Gilderbloom 1998, p. 71).

Literature related to elderly persons who are living alone indicates that type of neighborhood has an impact on access to social support. For example, Thompson and Krause (1998, p. 361) address the reality of elderly persons living alone and the reality or availability of social support. Their findings, resulting from 1,103 completed surveys with persons aged 65 to 99 who lived alone and with others, indicate three things about support system related to type of neighborhood: "neighborhood deterioration promotes fear of crime; fear of crime decreases the amount of emotional support elderly people receive [in general]; and more emotional support . . . increases anticipated support [from others]." In effect, the question of whether persons can remain in their own homes (and often do) should be determined in relation to the availability of support.

There is a small body of research related specifically to homosexuals and housing. For instance, the feasibility or lack thereof, of acquiring a place to live when one discloses his or her homosexuality has been explored by Page (1998). His study examined the effects of the homosexual label on the availability of rental property to persons who were open about their sexuality. Findings indicated, "reference to being homosexual in the telephoned enquiries . . . significantly decreased the likelihood of a room or flat being described as available" (Page 1998, p. 36). Page does clarify that embracing "the label" did not result in total rejection or total acceptance; however, it did have an effect on the availability of housing. Thus, the reality of maintaining a stigmatized label and its negative effects often proves detrimental when looking for a place to live.

Lucco (1987) has explored gay/lesbian respondents' desires in same-sex housing. This study was conducted with a volunteer sample of 57 lesbians and 399 gay men in which the mean age was 63.3 years. Interestingly, services that were the most desired included those of a sensitive staff, laundry facilities for personal use, and access to public transportation, while those features that were least desired included golf course, limousine service, and billiard room. Finally, McDonald (1998) interviewed 12 persons aged 53 to 84 years and found that gay men desired to have their own retirement housing. Presumably such housing would entail allowing elderly gay men to receive care that is sensitive to their specific needs and to be treated in a manner in which their lifestyle is appreciated or, at the very least, not negated or judged. The majority of respondents in the McDonald survey were single, so that an accommodation of persons in romantic partnerships was not mentioned; however, several respondents did indicate interest in a social support network that included a family of friends rather than blood relatives.

Other studies on the housing needs for gays and lesbians have been documented in the publication *Outword* (Kukoleck 1999). According to *Outword,* needs assessments, including the desire for same-sex housing, have been carried out in various cities such as Cleveland and Columbus, Philadelphia, Nashville, and Salt Lake City. This publication further reports that specific housing facilities are in the planning stages across the United States in cities such as San Francisco, Miami, Palm Springs, and Tampa. In addition, communities primarily for gay/lesbian people currently exist in the Palms of Manasota and in The Resort at Carefree Boulevard, both of which are located in Florida.

Also related specific to gay and lesbian persons and future housing needs, Cahill and colleagues (2000) have drafted a policy document related to the gay, lesbian, bisexual, and transgender community. In this document they indicate that the needs for the GLBT elderly are rooted in discriminatory practices, rather than lack of housing. Surprisingly, their recommendations are such that antidiscrimination policies affecting housing should include sexual orientation as a protected group. Although they indicate that a GLBT-specific housing facility will be nice, they do recognize that it will most likely not be affordable for all, so that the existence of affordable and integrated housing is more of a reality. Last, they indicate that staff at various housing facilities should be educated to respectfully work with GLBT seniors. As previously mentioned, there is no gay-specific housing in any of the four Texas cities where data have been collected. Moreover, although there have been discussions about needing such facilities in Dallas and Houston, no preliminary housing planning has taken place. It should be noted, however, that at the present time the only assisted or institutional living for homosexuals in Dallas is that provided by AIDS Services of Dallas.

THEORETICAL BASE

The grounded theory approach was used to frame information gathered from this research. Thus, although this study does not adhere to a specific theoretical base, it is important to mention existing and applicable theoretical frameworks.

Successful Aging

Several authors write about the concept of "successful aging," offering "models" for healthy and productive aging. Several of these models, however, incorporate more than mere physical or psychological health. By way of illustration, Rowe and Kahn

(1997) have developed a model for successful aging that includes the avoidance of disease and disability; a maintenance of engagement with life; and maintenance of functioning, both at the cognitive and physical levels. The implications of their model include the idea that "many of the predictors of risk and of both functional and activity levels appear to be potentially modifiable, either by individuals or by changes in their immediate environments" so that interventions can be created for the person who presumably is not having a successful aging experience (Rowe and Kahn 1997, p. 439). The thought of aging successfully is vital as we approach record numbers of elderly living within our society. For persons who are homosexual, however, successful aging would presumably take into account their sexuality.

Friend (1991) has developed a theoretical model for successful aging specific to gay and lesbian people. This tripartite model is composed of the following dimensions: individual psychology, social and interpersonal dimensions, and legal and political advocacy. For the realm of individual psychology, Friend (1991) asserts personal "success" when homosexual identity is accepted. In addition to accepting one's identity as a homosexual, the individual must also be comfortable with gender and age identity. Family and friends create a happy and healthy social and interpersonal dimension so that the person is neither isolated nor alone. Last, the avoidance of victimization based on age or homosexuality is important. These unpleasant realities can be navigated by maintaining an awareness of rights and responsibilities affecting the gay community. Recognizing and standing against injustice can prevent victimization. Thus, successful aging within this theoretical model presupposes continued life engagement and a mastering of experience within each realm.

By contrast, proponents of disengagement theory assert that aging entails withdrawal from various aspects of social life (see Moody 1998). This theory which suggests the opposite of Friend's "successful aging," such that as persons age, they become more and more withdrawn from the world around them. There are little data to suggest whether this is the case with homosexuals.

Finally, any research with the gay population must take into account the importance of the social stigma still associated with this way of life. Goffman (1963) documents the role of stigma and the way that individuals and society deal with various stigmatizing attributes. Negative stereotypes regarding the aging gay man have been documented (Kelly 1977; Berger 1996; Slusher et al. 1996). The stigma associated with these negative images is something that aging gay men have to face. Blumer (1969) wrote about the importance of symbolic interaction and how we create our realities based on interpretation, negotiation, and continued involvement in the exchange of symbols and their meanings. This theoretical framework was useful for understanding the realities of participants in this study.

Again, it was the purpose of this research to describe the life situations of aging gay men so that the lives which these men live on a daily basis can be understood. How the men are coping, or plan to cope, with the aging experience in relation to their homosexuality was also explored. Comparisons were made with the existing literature so that the process of aging for some homosexual men in some Texas cities can be addressed as the process relates to data collected in other parts of the country and during other periods of time. Although the grounded theoretical approach is the primary framework for this study, existing, relevant theoretical perspectives, where appropriate, were also utilized.

SUMMARY

This chapter has described existing literature in the major areas included in this research: health and well-being, social support/relationships/involvement, and housing. In addition, the process of aging has been reviewed as it relates to both heterosexuals and homosexuals, as has a review of sociological theory, which will be utilized to frame the findings of this study. The next chapter describes the methods used in data collection.

Chapter 3

Methodology

This study is exploratory in nature, including both quantitative and qualitative dimensions. Therefore, testing of formal hypotheses is not appropriate.

RESEARCH QUESTIONS

This study was guided by the use of major research questions, which is appropriate for descriptive sociological research (Berg 2001; Lofland and Lofland 1995). The selected research questions pertain to the actual life experiences that gay men undergo as they age as homosexuals and were designed to collect data describing the physical, mental, and social needs of the men. The research questions guiding this study follow:

1. What are the housing needs of the aging gay male community?
   - What housing needs are anticipated in the future?
2. How do aging gay men describe their health and well-being?
   - Do aging gay men consider themselves to be physically healthy?
   - Do members of this population perceive themselves as suffering from depression?
   - If they do consider themselves to be depressed, what do they perceive as the cause?

3. Do members of this group have access to social support networks?
4. How involved are aging gay men with family, friends, church, and community?

DEFINITIONS

For this study, "aging" or "elderly" were used interchangeably to refer to persons who are at least 55 years of age. "Gay" and "homosexual" were used to signify men who self-identify (for purposes of this research) as having emotional and sexual relationships with other men. The concept of "health and well-being" (physical and mental) was derived from a series of questions in which the respondents' perceptions of well-being were solicited. Several questions relevant to the availability of friends or family were used as a measure of "social support." Certain "needs," such as housing, were based on the participants' perceptions. Last, "involvement" was ascertained by participants' reported membership and participation in community and church organizations.

RESEARCH PARTICIPANTS

The criteria used in the selection of the sample were twofold: (1) respondents were chosen by their sex and sexual orientation (gay or bisexual);* and (2) respondents were age 55 or older. Due to the small sample size and the nature of this study, the sample is not representative. However, because so little information is available on this population, any data are valuable in contributing to an understanding and knowledge about aging among gay males. Participants in the quantitative component portion of the research study consisted of 125 men in four cities who completed and re-

---

*Being gay and being bisexual are two entirely different identities and lifestyles. However, it was not the focus of this research to delineate the variations. This study was aimed at discovering how persons deal with a stigmatizing label as a sexual minority and navigate the aging process. The project was advertised as such and participants were allowed to self-identify and take part in the study if they so desired.

turned survey forms. Twenty of these men from Dallas also partic-ipated in the qualitative portion of the research by volunteering to be interviewed.

DATA COLLECTION

Survey Instrument

Participants responded to an eight-page questionnaire (see Ap-pendix B) designed specifically for this project to solicit reactions to the experience of aging as a gay male. Specifically, questions were arranged into sections. The four major sections on the survey in-cluded questions related to (1) social support/relationships/involve-ment; (2) housing; (3) health and well-being; and (4) employment. Responses to these questions were generally structured, resulting in quantitative data. However, several questions were open-ended so that the men were able to respond in their own words. Thus, qualitative data also resulted from the survey instrument. Ques-tions contained in these four sections were created to answer the research questions guiding this study. Two additional sections in-cluded a concluding thoughts section and a demographics section. Here, the men were asked to report some limited demographic in-formation, whether they have any regrets about the way their lives have turned out, and what, if anything, is left on their "to-do" lists. Pilot tests of the survey instrument were conducted with two men and minor changes were then made to the document. Both men who participated in the pretest fit the criteria for inclusion in the study; however they were not resurveyed in the final project.

Quantitative Component

The quantitative component of this study is made up of 125 completed surveys. Of this total, 35 (28 percent) were from Aus-tin, 49 (39.2 percent) were from Dallas, 14 (11.2 percent) were from Houston, and 27 (21.6 percent) were from San Antonio. Sur-vey data were collected in several ways and varied from city to city. However, the primary means of data collection in each city was through the Prime Timers Worldwide organization. After initial contacts, facilitated by the founding member of Prime Timers, each city's Prime Timers chapter wrote something about this study in its monthly newsletter. Over a three-month period, each city was visited and a monthly meeting was attended, and by this time potential respondents knew of the study. At each meeting the research study was described and surveys were distributed. Some men completed surveys at the meeting, and others mailed them back.

Data for this part of the study were collected over a three-and one-half-month period—December 17, 2000, through March 31, 2001. The men who completed surveys were guaranteed both confidentiality and anonymity. A cover letter explained that completion and return of the survey instrument granted permission to utilize the information. The letter informed respondents that participation was voluntary and that all information would remain confidential. Table 4.1 in the next chapter shows general demographic characteristics of persons taking part in this component of the study.

The Search for Participants

Initially, contacts were made with men in each of the four cities via Prime Timers Worldwide. This is an organization whose purpose is to

> provide mature gay and bisexual men, and their admirers, with opportunities to come together in a supportive atmosphere in order to enrich their lives with social, educational, and recreational activities. (Original Prime Timers Worldwide 2000)

Woody Baldwin founded the organization in Boston, Massachusetts, in 1987. Currently there are 50 chapters worldwide, located throughout North America, Europe, and Australia. Entrée was granted through the founding member of Prime Timers Worldwide, who now resides in Austin, Texas. Later, different contact persons were introduced via snowball sampling so that after initial contacts were made with respondents, other potential respondents were introduced who could be interviewed and/or surveyed in the community. This kind of strategy is described by Berg (2001) as the "snowball effect."

Four Cities

Dallas. Because of previous work in the Dallas gay community, numerous contacts in the city were already known and reliance on the Prime Timers organization was not heavy. Personal friendship networks and a local health club that is frequented by predominantly gay and lesbian persons provided added research participants. Work on another research project with the Resource Center of Dallas, a gay/lesbian community center, provided contact with potential respondents as well. Finally, attendance at the primarily gay/lesbian church in Dallas contributed some respondents to the study.

A meeting of the Dallas Prime Timers organization was attended by the researcher on December 17, 2000, in the Resource Center of Dallas. At this meeting, several things were observed. Most notably, only one man appeared to be under 50 years of age. He was 21 years old and was the significant other of an older member of the group. There was only one African American in the group, and no one who appeared to be Latino or Asian American was present. Members were cordial and seemed to be interested in the study. There were approximately 50 members present and everyone wore nametags. This is a very social group with only four business meetings per year (in which committee reports are given, minutes are read, etc.). They have from five to ten social outings per month, including dinners, brunches, potlucks, and bowling and movie nights. At the December 2000 meeting, 34 surveys were distributed.

The researcher attended three services of the Dallas Metropolitan Community Church, the Cathedral of Hope. This church is primarily for gay and lesbian people and is reported to be the largest gay/lesbian religious congregation in the world. The three services (at 8:30 a.m., 10 a.m., and 11:30 a.m.) were attended on February 11, 2001. In this setting, a table was set up in the narthex of the church so that those interested in participating were able to stop by either before or after each service to pick up a survey. The church leaders were helpful in putting a note in the bulletin. When virtually no one had stopped by the table after the first service, the pastor was asked if he would make an announcement during the next two services. He agreed and did this for the 10 a.m. services after which several surveys were distributed. He forgot to mention the study during the third service, however, and few were distributed at that time. Ushers reported that seating capacity of the sanctuary is roughly 800 persons. Total distribution in this venue was about 20 surveys.

Other methods of distribution in Dallas included ten surveys that were given to a friend who has acquaintances who fit the criteria for inclusion in the study. About five persons who heard of this study either through the church or other participants solicited surveys themselves. One other person was met in an online chat room and he agreed to participate in the survey, and one was mailed to him. The total number of surveys distributed in Dallas, at the Prime Timers meeting, the three church services, and through a contact person was 70, with a return rate of 70 percent, or 49 surveys.

San Antonio. The researcher attended meetings of the San Antonio Prime Timers organization two times. The first time was a Christmas breakfast on December 25, 2000. This was not an ideal situation to collect data because the setting was a private home. During the breakfast, the president of the organization made an announcement about the study and several men took surveys; however, the number distributed was less than 20. Observations at this meeting included the fact that only one African-American man was present in the group. He looked to be about 30 years old. Few persons looked to be under 50 years of age. There were roughly 50 to 60 persons in attendance.

San Antonio was revisited on January 14, 2001, for another meeting of the Prime Timers. This time, the group met in the dining hall of that city's Metropolitan Community Church. The venue was a general meeting and a chili cook-off. Again, food and socialization were the main agenda, and completion of surveys was not the top priority of those in attendance. General observations at this time included the fact those that there were about 40 men present, but no African Americans or Asian Americans. One member did look Latino, although this was not confirmed. At this time, ten surveys were completed and returned, while the remainder was left for respondents to complete at home and mail back. Again, less than 20 surveys were distributed. Ten surveys were left for the president, who said he had friends and family who fit the criteria and were not Prime Timers.

San Antonio was visited again on March 9, 2001, and a meeting with the president of the Prime Timers was held on March 10, 2001. At this time, a letter of consent to visit the organization's meetings was obtained. During this visit, conversation ensued about the progress of the study and ten more surveys were left for the president to distribute to persons who fit the criteria for inclusion. The total number of surveys distributed in San Antonio (including the two sets of ten that were left with the president on two different occasions) was 44, with a return rate of 61.3 percent, or 27 surveys.

Houston. Houston was visited on January 13, 2001. The Prime Timers meeting there was held in the "club room" of the president's condominium complex. At this meeting, the researcher for this project was the featured speaker; thus, the talk was a bit longer than it was in the other locations. Attendance at the meeting, however, was low, with only 15 men present. Because the subject of the meeting was announced in advance, perhaps knowledge of the survey to be presented might have kept persons away if they did not want to participate in the research. Some did complete the surveys at the meeting, and others chose to take the survey with them. There were no African Americans or Asian Americans present. There was one Latino in attendance. Also, only one member looked to be less than 55 years of age. The number of surveys distributed in Houston was 29, with a return rate of 48.2 percent, or 14 surveys.

Austin. On March 11, 2001, the researcher attended the Metropolitan Community Church at Freedom Oaks, which is Austin's gay/lesbian church. In speaking with ushers the researcher learned that the ratio of men to women who attend the church is about one to one, and the seating capacity of the sanctuary is 280 to 300 persons. The church has been experiencing rapid growth and attracts 12 to 15 new members each week; the racial makeup of persons who attend is predominantly white. The pastor announced the research during the announcements period in the service (at which time he introduced the researcher) and again at the end of the service. The study and visit were also documented in the church bulletin. Roughly ten surveys were distributed at this time.

In addition to the church service, the Austin Prime Timers meeting was attended on the same day. At this meeting, the researcher was permitted to speak for about ten minutes. There was also a featured speaker in addition to the business of conducting board member elections. There were approximately 25 persons present including one African-American man and two persons who looked Asian. There were two to five persons who looked to be under 50 years of age, while everyone else looked older than that. Again, the meeting was very social, with 30 minutes devoted to eating and socializing. At this venue, about 40 surveys were distributed; however, 12 of those went to one person who indicated that he had a circle of friends who fit the criteria for inclusion and were not in attendance. Two surveys were completed at the meeting and returned. The return rate for this city was 70 percent, or 35 surveys.

Problems with Data Collection

Some problems in retrieving completed surveys from all cities included: (1) Prime Timers meetings are very social, and members were not necessarily focused on completing the survey at the time of the meeting, although some did. (2) Both the Houston and San Antonio meetings were centered on food, so that members were less inclined to sit and complete the survey. The Dallas meeting was very organized (with committee reports and a formal program) so that although attendees were not distracted by food and conversation, they were focused on the formality of the meeting and not necessarily on completing the survey. The Austin meeting was also a bit more formal; however, the arrangement of the room (with chairs arranged in an "audience" fashion) was not conducive to completing the survey. (3) A stamped return envelope was not provided. Although this was acknowledged at the time the survey was distributed and people were asked to help by donating a stamp, not providing a stamp may have negatively affected the return rate.

Qualitative Component

In-depth interviews were used as a qualitative source of data. Prior to each interview and after studying each completed survey, an interview guide was constructed. This enabled probing for more detail and depth than was available in the data collected via the completed surveys. The interview guide was arranged in the same order as the survey. The participants were first asked to elaborate on or to clarify responses about social support/relationships/involvement, then health and well-being, and finally, employment. However, each interview guide was tailored to each respondent, based on answers given on the survey. Specific questions were posed to the interviewees, some of which related directly to the research questions guiding this study and some (for example, the question of how, or if, the Internet has affected the life of the respondent) were posed to discover possible changes that are being experienced by this cohort of aging gay men. The interview guide offered the opportunity to probe the realities of aging gay men with regard to their living situations, their mental and physical health, and their social support networks. This interview guide was a point of departure. Frequent probes with follow-up questions and comments relating to the problems faced and issues encountered as an aging gay man occurred. A sample interview schedule is included in Appendix B.

Interviews were conducted with the first 20 respondents from Dallas who completed the survey and indicated a willingness to be part of the qualitative component of this study. Qualitative data drawn from in-depth interviews were ideal for gaining insight into the social phenomenon of aging gay men and for a better understanding of the issues surrounding the aging process as experienced by men who are homosexuals. The first qualitative interview was conducted on January 7, 2001, and the last was conducted on March 23, 2001. All of the respondents were guaranteed confidentiality. All were assured that the researcher would be the only person collecting the data for this project, transcribing the interview tapes, analyzing the data, and writing the findings and conclusions. Consent, by means of a formal consent form, was obtained from all respondents to audiotape as well as to take notes during the interviews. Respondents were informed that the interviews were confidential and voluntary.

The respondents for this component were asked questions that related to responses given on their completed surveys. Thus, it was possible to probe, to ask clarifying questions, and to go into detail about data obtained on the survey. In addition all respondents were asked some questions that were not on the survey. These questions were as follows:

1. Socially, do you feel involved and fulfilled, or do you feel alone?
2. Currently, what do you perceive the housing needs of the aging gay male community to be?
3. What do you think the housing needs of aging gay men will be in the future?
4. If you were to need social support in the Dallas area, either related to being gay or your age or your gender, are you aware of services that are available to you?
5. Do you have a large circle of friends?
6. Would you say you are very social or somewhat shy?
7. How has the Internet affected your life, if at all?
8. Can you describe a typical week?

The actual formal interviews, which were recorded on audiotape, ranged from 20 to 90 minutes. Interviews were scheduled by telephone, e-mail, or in person, after the respondents indicated a willingness to participate in this capacity via the completed survey. All interview appointments were made at the convenience of the respondents. Interviews were typically conducted at the homes of respondents and at times convenient for them. Three respondents came to the home of the researcher and one person was interviewed at a university office. Two couples were interviewed, and the remainder of the persons were either single or in relationships. General observations gleaned from the interviews included the fact that the respondents live in all sorts of housing and in various types of relationships with significant others. The persons interviewed were generally very friendly. On a few occasions the researcher was given a tour of respondents' homes; on other occasions respondents showed the researcher their hobbies, family photos, etc. Sometimes redirection of the interview was needed after respondents took phone calls. None of the scheduled interviews was missed or had to be rescheduled. All interview participants were very cooperative and had no problems in responding to the questions.

DATA PROCESSING AND ANALYSIS

Data were derived from completed surveys (N = 125) and in-depth interviews (N = 20). Quantitative and demographic data were drawn from the completed surveys. Qualitative data primarily were derived from the in-depth interviews with the respondents from the Dallas area. (However, it should be noted that some qualitative questions were included in the survey and have been utilized to provide supplemental information to the quantitative data.) The surveys were coded with a number to indicate from which city they came. Each survey was numbered consecutively. All data collected were coded in a way that is understandable to the researcher yet meaningless to anyone else to ensure confidentiality. For instance, the typed transcripts, consent forms, notes from the in-depth interviews, and completed surveys were coded with city numbers in addition to survey numbers. The key containing the code was stored in a place that no one else had access to and was destroyed after the study was completed.

Quantitative Data

Surveys were coded and entered into SPSS, a statistical software package, for the compilation of descriptive statistics. Because of nonrandom sampling, this study does not aim to test hypotheses, and measures of association or test of significance are not appropriate for these data. Demographic information listed for the respondents were reported along with frequencies and percentages on each of the survey items related to the research questions. Cross-tabulation tables of some items were generated in order to look at possible associations.

Qualitative Data

Gubrium and Holstein (1995) document the utility of biographical work and the narrative process for understanding the life course of individuals. Their work on life course is qualitative and makes use of the in-depth interview as this research has done. In asserting the utility of qualitative data collection, Gubrium and Holstein indicate

> Narrative linkage can operate at the very start of storytelling, acting as a kind of preface to narration. It does not simply emerge to structure distinct meaning as a story unfolds but can be used reflexively to signal possible coherences. (1998, p. 168)

They also assert:

> Narrative analysis refers loosely to the examination of the diverse stories, commentaries, and the conversations engaged in everyday life. Ethnography points broadly to the careful and usually long-term observation of a group of people to reveal the patterns of social life that are locally experienced. (Gubrium and Holstein 1999, p. 561)

This study is not an ethnography, but the data-collection techniques are similar and the methods for data analysis are related as well.

To begin the analysis, each transcript was read for an initial content analysis. Notes were written in the margins about major themes; interesting quotes and various patterns that emerged from specific responses were noted (Berg 2001). Interesting and representative quotes to illustrate the themes were marked. After all of the transcripts were read and notations made, the data were more systematically coded and themes were organized around a specific research question. However, the transcripts, the coding, and the data analysis proceeded in the same manner that the survey instrument and interview guide were formulated, so that data related to social support were organized together, data related to health and well-being were organized together, etc. Again, qualitative data were coded and organized thematically, so that the guiding research questions could be answered from the conversations engaged in with respondents (Berg 2001).

More specifically related to the use of thematic analysis, Spradley (1979) mentions the extraction of "universal themes" in analyzing qualitative data as these themes relate to the larger part of the respondent's reality, such as social conflict or cultural contradictions. The primary themes identified in these data were those to emerge in responses to specific questions, so that both similarities and differences were noted. Again, specific quotes were extracted from the transcripts to illustrate qualitative data where appropriate. Major themes and subthemes were extracted by examining responses to specific questions and grouping similar responses. These themes taken together were examined for the "universal themes" identified by Spradley (1980, p. 152). Narrative responses were sought to illuminate the life situations of respondents in this study (see Lofland and Lofland 1995). Specifically, the words of the respondents were used appropriately to document personal situations and experiences that could be generalized to others taking part in this research. Quotes used in Chapter 4 are representative of themes that emerged in response to specific interview questions.

PROTECTION OF PARTICIPANTS

As previously stated, permission was obtained to tape each interview and to take notes. All of the respondents were assured of the fact that the researcher would be the only one to transcribe the tapes and to analyze the data. Thus, everyone appeared to feel comfortable discussing the issues at hand. Identifiable traits of the interviewees were altered to protect them from possible detection and identification in any quotes used. For example, no names are used in the analysis, and only descriptive data that identifies such things as age and occupation are offered.

Moral and ethical issues associated with qualitative research as set forth in Berg's (2001) text were apparent at all times. At no time were any of the respondents placed in danger or at risk due to participation in this research project. Because of the specific population being addressed, issues surrounding the gay community were apparent and personal judgments or values were not conveyed to respondents.

SUMMARY

This chapter describes the methodology utilized in collecting data for this study. The number of total surveys collected in various ways from four cities was 125. The primary source for data collection was the Prime Timers Worldwide organization in four cities. In addition, two gay churches were visited, and personal contacts were utilized for some survey distribution. Of the total number of men returning surveys in Dallas, the first 20 volunteering to be interviewed were contacted and interviewed for more in-depth information regarding their survey responses. Other specific questions were asked of these men only.

The next chapter describes sample characteristics and addresses the research questions. Both quantitative and qualitative data are used to illuminate responses to each research question and to provide a better understanding of the aging gay male experience.

Chapter 4

Findings

This chapter presents demographic characteristics of the men who took part in this study, both those who returned surveys and those who gave personal interviews. Findings have been organized around research questions and all relevant quantitative and qualitative data are presented on each.

RESPONDENT CHARACTERISTICS

Survey Respondents

Table 4.1 lists the demographic characteristics of all respondents who returned surveys for this research. The total sample size was 125. There were no appreciable differences among residents in each of the four cities, except for heterosexual marriage experience in the case of the Austin respondents. The table appearing in Appendix A lists the attributes of participants by city.

Of 123 persons providing information related to their sexual orientation, the vast majority (92 percent), when asked if they were gay, bisexual, or heterosexual, said they were homosexual. Most respondents had no previous experience with a heterosexual marriage; for those that had been married, length of time married ranged from six months to 42 years. For the 122 respondents who answered the question about whether they had children, over two-thirds (68.8 percent) said they did not. Participants reported a total of 83 children, ranging from one to six per participant, with children's ages ranging from 15 to 57.

TABLE 4.1. Demographics of Survey Participants

Characteristic	N	Percent
Age	124	99.2
Range: 55-84 years		
Mean: 65 years		
Median: 63 years		
Race/Ethnicity		
White	115	92.0
African American	2	1.6
Latino	4	3.2
American Indian	1	0.8
Other	2	1.6
Missing	1	0.8
Sexuality		
Homosexual/gay	115	92.0
Bisexual	8	6.4
Missing	2	1.6
Level of Education		
High school	14	11.2
Some college/Associate's	19	15.2
Bachelor's degree	35	28.0
Master's degree	36	28.8
PhD/professional	19	15.2
Missing	2	1.6
Heterosexual Marriage		
Yes	45	36.0
No	80	64.0
Children		
Yes	36	28.8
No	86	68.8
Missing	3	2.4

The educational attainment of respondents ranged from completion of high school to those with a doctorate or other professional degrees (such as MD, JD, DDS, etc.). Interestingly, 28 percent of participants had bachelor's degrees and almost 29 percent had received a master's degree. The vast majority (92 percent) self-identified as white/Caucasian/European American.

Interviewees

Table 4.2 presents the characteristics of those who participated in the interview part of this study. The age of participants for the interview varied from 55 to 78 years. They were all white men who identified as homosexual or gay. The majority held a bachelor's degree or better (60 percent) and had no previous experience with a heterosexual marriage (75 percent). None of the interviewees was currently married. Of those who had been married (N = 5) the length of time varied from five to 42 years. Specifically, one person had been married for five years, two had been married from

TABLE 4.2. Demographics of Interview Participants

Characteristics	N	Percent
Age	20	100.0
Range: 55-78 years Mean: 62.9 years Median: 63.0 years		
Race/Ethnicity		
White	20	100.0
Sexuality		
Homosexual/gay	20	100.0
Level of Education		
High school	3	15.0
Some college/Associate's	5	25.0
Bachelor's degree	7	35.0
Master's degree	4	20.0
PhD/professional	1	5.0
Heterosexual Marriage		
Yes	5	25.0
No	15	75.0
Children		
Yes	6	30.0
No	13	65.0
Missing	1	5.0

21 to 23 years, and the other two persons had been married from 40 to 42 years. For the six persons who said they had children, five gave ages of their children which ranged from 33 to 46. In addition, two said they had three children, three said they had two children, and one did not give this information.

SOCIAL SUPPORT, RELATIONSHIPS, AND INVOLVEMENT OF RESPONDENTS

Research questions related to available social support and involvement follow: (1) How involved are aging gay men with family, friends, church, and community? (2) Do members of this group have access to social support networks? Responses were collected in various ways.

Interview respondents were asked only whether they knew of available social support in the Dallas area, should they need it. The majority did. Again, because this was a socially connected group of men, they cited church as a resource or previous experience with volunteer work and organizations as sources for help. In cases where participants lacked firsthand knowledge of places to go for social support, they mentioned knowing whom to call to ask for this type of information. Specifically, respondents said, "Yes. Yes, it's out there" and, "I think so." Another said of agencies for gay persons, "I know there are; I've had friends who've gone to a couple of places, but I've not looked into it." The exception to this type of response was a person who recently moved to Dallas, who said, "Zero. The only one that I know of is support for AIDS victims."

Survey participants were asked basic questions pertaining to their interpersonal relationships. These data are presented in Table 4.3. This table shows that more participants (46.4 percent) were in committed relationships than were single (43.2 percent) or casually dating (4.8 percent). Five respondents checked the "Other" category in this section of the survey. Interestingly, four of the five were from Austin, with reasons for checking this category being "sex buddy" relationship; married to a woman; "widow" of gay lover; and one person indicated he was semicommitted to one person while dating another. The fifth person said he had a heterosexual wife and a male lover. Length of time for being in a committed relationship varied from under one to 63 years, with a mean of almost 22 years. Persons who were single had been so from under one year to 76 years, with a mean of just over 21 years. For purposes of presentation, when respondents gave time in years, these were reduced to numbers of months, then back to years. Also, for those who said they had been single "forever" or "all my life," 18 years were subtracted from the age of the respondent and the number of months then calculated based on number of years. The age of 18 served as a way to standardize the "adult" experience, as it was assumed this

TABLE 4.3. Interpersonal Relationships/Involvement of Survey Participants

Relationship Information		N	Percent
		125	100.0
Relationship Status			
Single		54	43.2
Casually dating		6	4.8
In a committed relationship		58	46.4
Other		5	4.0
Missing		2	1.6
Length of Time			
Single		54	43.2
Mean years	21		
Range in years	0-76		
Casually Dating		6	4.8
Mean years	53		
Range in years	0-1		
In Committed Relationship		5	46.4
Mean years	22		
Range in years	0-63		
Other		5	4.0
Mean years	25		
Range in years	3-45		
Missing		2	1.6

would be the time that the men began to pursue romantic relationships, either heterosexual or homosexual.

Because for many the church is known to be a primary support group, respondents were asked about church involvement or religiosity. These data are presented in Table 4.4. Church attendance was reported by the majority (60 percent) of respondents. Moreover, and most (73.3 percent) said they did so on a regular basis. The majority of respondents were Protestant (52.8 percent), with the next largest category having no religious affiliation (17.6 percent). A majority of respondents evaluated their "religious convictions" as either strong (34.4 percent) or somewhat strong (20.0 percent). Almost 20 percent said they did not have very strong religious con-

TABLE 4.4. Church/Religious Involvement of Survey Participants

Characteristic	N	Percent
Church Attendance		
Yes	75	60.0
No	49	39.2
Missing	1	0.8
Regularity of Attendance		
Regular	55	73.3
Irregular	20	26.7
Religious Preference		
Protestant	66	52.8
Catholic	16	12.8
Jewish	4	3.2
None	22	17.6
Other	14	11.2
Don't know	1	0.8
Missing	2	1.6
Strong Religious Convictions		
Strong	43	34.4
Somewhat strong	25	20.0
Not very strong	24	19.2
No religion	12	9.6
Don't know	2	1.6
N/A	15	12.0
Missing	4	3.2

TABLE 4.5. Group/Social Organization Involvement of Survey Participants

Activity Item	N	Percent
Group/Organization Activity		
Yes	102	81.6
No	23	18.4
Level of Participation		
Very active	46	45.1
Moderately active	44	43.1
Not very active	12	11.8

victions, and only 10 percent reported having no religious convictions.

Table 4.5 documents the respondents' involvements with various groups or organizations. The majority (81.6 percent) of respondents were socially active. This is not surprising, since the method used for collecting these data (i.e., membership in Prime Timers) predetermined some level of social involvement. The respondents' reported activities varied among Prime Timers chapters; however, city choirs, various church organizations, garden clubs, car clubs, business or political groups, and book clubs were typical social activities. Levels of activity ranged from very active to not very active, with almost 90 percent indicating they were very or moderately active; under 12 percent reported that they were not very active.

Respondents were asked about their dating activities because, for single persons, dating is likely to be an important part of social involvement. In interviews, many talked about the desire for coupling and dating. However, it was not unusual for these interviewees to indicate a desire to couple yet not date very much. In those instances, respondents indicated such reasons as "I'm too old to date," "I'm too old to couple," "I could never live with someone again/now." One respondent in particular said of dating,

I don't. It's hard for people in this age bracket to meet people. I'm attracted to older guys. Really, I like guys over forty and most of these people are pretty cautious. And it takes a lot to meet people.

Another respondent who did not actively date blamed his work schedule:

Time, mainly. I travel a lot and it's very difficult to maintain any kind of relationship when you're on the road oh, two or three weeks out of four. If I were in town, very consistently, I might work toward that goal, but right now, it's just not there.

Table 4.6 illustrates dating characteristics of participants. Survey respondents were split between those who did date and those who did not. Almost 30 percent in both cases did date (29.6 percent) and did not date (27.2 percent). Thirty-four persons responded to the question about frequency of dating, and most said they dated once a month (51.4 percent) with the next greatest frequency being once a week (21.6 percent). These data are not necessarily exclusive of persons who reported being single. Several persons who are coupled reported dating their partner and indicated how often they went out on movie or dinner dates.

Relevant to their social relationships and involvements, respondents were asked questions about their friends and families. These data are reported in Tables 4.7 and 4.8. For example, over one-half

TABLE 4.6. Dating Characteristics of Survey Participants

Characteristic	N	Percent
Dating Relationships		
Yes	37	29.6
No	34	27.2
Missing	54	43.2
Dating Frequency		
Once a year	4	10.8
Once a month	19	51.4
Once a week	8	21.6
More than once a week	3	8.1
Missing	3	8.1

(54.4 percent) of respondents said their friends are mostly gay, and 40 percent indicated that their friends are a mix of both homosexuals and heterosexuals. Over one-half (55.2 percent) of respondents said they have a surrogate family of friends who have replaced blood relatives, and 44 percent said they did not. Respondents were also asked about whether they experienced difficulty meeting others for friends or dates. Here, the majority (60.8 percent) said they did not experience any difficulty, and almost one-third said they did. One interview respondent, who was in a relationship and indicated that he did not experience difficulty meeting others, was queried about where he met people for social interaction. He said, "We go to the Cathedral of Hope and we've met a lot of people through that. And we got a lot of friends, who, you know, they have circles." Another person, who was single and indicated difficulty meeting others, referred to compatibility and said of his difficulties,

> I would like somebody on my collegiate level, same job level, same income level, so there could be some equality there. But it's hard to meet people, especially moving into a big city like this.

Finally, one person succinctly said,

> Well, for gay people, you . . . have two ways of meeting. . . . You either network through other friends or you can meet people at the bars. And through there [bars] ultimately you can get networked and you meet people.

When asked if friends were older or younger (or a mix) than the respondent the majority (72.8 percent) said a mix, almost 5 percent said older, and over 22 percent said younger.

Data related to sibling relationships are also included in Table 4.7. Eighty percent of respondents reported having brothers and sisters, while 20 percent said they did not. When asked about whether they had a close relationship with siblings, over half (58 percent)

TABLE 4.7. Friend and Family Relationships of Survey Participants

Characteristic	N	Percent
Sexual Orientation of Friends		
Mostly gay	68	54.4
Mostly nongay	6	4.8
Mix of both	50	40.0
Missing	1	0.8
Friends Replacing Blood Relatives		
Yes	69	55.2
No	55	44.0
Missing	1	0.8
Difficulty Meeting Others		
Yes	40	32.0
No	76	60.8
Missing	9	7.2
Age of Friends		
Older	6	4.8
Younger	28	22.4
Mix of both	91	72.8
Siblings		
Yes	100	80.0
No	25	20.0
Close Relationship with Siblings		
Yes	58	58.0
No	30	30.0
With one or some but not all	12	12.0

(N = 100) said they did, while just under one-third said they did not. In addition, 12 percent said they did have a close relationship with one or some siblings, but not all. In the survey, one respondent said that he was not close to his siblings. During the interview I asked why. His reply was that he had a sister and a brother and that the only sibling he was estranged from was his brother. When I asked about the closeness to the brother, he said, "No. Not at all." He failed to elaborate and I asked if it had anything to do with his homosexuality and he said, "They don't even know I'm gay." The respondent seemed unwilling to discuss the details of his estrangement from the brother and I did not continue to probe.

Disclosure information is located in Table 4.8. Of the 124 responding to the question regarding whether they were "out" to family, over half (50.4 percent) said they were, while 28 percent said they were not, and almost 21 percent said they were out to some members of their family. One respondent, who was not out to his family, said during the interview, "Why should I be? I look at sexual orientation as a very small part of who we are. It has nothing to do with anything, I don't think." All 125 respondents answered the question regarding whether they were out to friends with more than half (52.8 percent) reporting they were out, while under 5 percent said they were not, and just over 42 percent said they were out to some but not all of their friends. The question relating to co-workers showed the most variety with regard to open-

TABLE 4.8. Disclosure Status of Survey Participants

Characteristic	N	Percent
Disclosure to Family		
Yes	63	50.4
No	35	28.0
Out to some	26	20.8
Missing	1	0.8
Disclosure to Friends		
Yes	66	52.8
No	6	4.8
Out to some	53	42.4
Disclosure to Co-Workers		
Yes	33	26.4
No	37	29.6
Out to some	32	25.6
Missing	23	18.4
Support Loss Due to Disclosure of Homosexuality		
Yes	27	21.6
No	97	77.6
Missing	1	0.8

ness. This is not surprising given that homophobic policies or attitudes often manifest in work environments, causing concerns about job security. Over 25 percent of persons responding said they were out to co-workers while 29.6 said they were not out and 25.6 said they were out to some. Those persons who were not out to co-workers seemed to rationalize or perceive their lack of disclosure in terms of a professional ethic. That is, they chose not to disclose personal information at work, but did not feel stigmatized due to their homosexuality, although one person did say, when asked why he was not out,

> Fear, probably. The business that I'm in is a very macho business, in the sense that I deal a lot with guys who are in their twenties who are probably not terribly secure in their sexuality in some cases and for me to come out as a gay person to them would have. . . . There'd be nothing positive . . . It would not engender any good feelings.

Another respondent who said he was not out to co-workers and out to only some friends, said of his co-workers, "Well, it's not that— well, I don't go around telling people. I don't discuss my life with them and they don't discuss their life with me. It's not something we discuss." Of not being out to all his friends, he said,

> Oh, I'd say any close friends are aware. They know what my life has been. I don't think any intelligent person, if they know somebody's in their sixties and they've never been involved with a person of the opposite sex, particularly, and they're always with a person of their own sex, I don't think it needs to be discussed. They know. If not, they're not very intelligent.

Not all respondents replied to the question related to being out at work because many were retired or not working. Regarding whether persons had lost the support of someone to whom they had divulged their homosexuality, over three-fourths (77.6 percent) said they had not, while almost 22 percent said they had.

Interview respondents who indicated having lost the support of someone due to disclosure of their homosexuality were asked a follow-up question. One respondent said that he had lost the support of his family.

> Well, they all knew. Most of my family knew that I was gay, but they didn't have anything to do with me. They wouldn't call me or write me or they wouldn't invite me over.

Those men participating in the interview were asked not only clarifying questions about the survey but also other questions, such as: Socially, do you feel involved and fulfilled, or do you feel alone? Do you have a large circle of friends? Are you very social or somewhat shy? and, If you were to need social support in the Dallas area, either related to being gay, your age, or your gender, are you aware of services that are available to you? One respondent who is 58, single, and recently moved from Oklahoma said that he felt "Alone. Very much so." When asked about his circle of friends, he said that he had a large circle in Oklahoma, but not in Dallas. In fact, his reason for joining Prime Timers was to become more involved with friends. He had lived in Dallas for only seven months prior to the interview. Another single respondent said

> Involved and fulfilled. We all have periods of "Gee, I wish . . ." you know, "I'd like to go chat with somebody," but mainly I feel pretty much involved. Fulfilled. All kinds of interesting things to do.

This respondent also stated that although he had a large circle of friends, he considered himself to be somewhat shy. A person who was in a relationship and had been for 31 years answered the question regarding social involvement:

> No, I feel very involved. We have a very good social life. With a lot of our friends and a lot of our gay friends, but also

we have a very involved social life with [my partner's] family and my family as well. And we're very socially active in both aspects.

With regard to the question related to social support in the Dallas area, this same respondent said that he did not know of any specifically, but he does know such support exists.

The guiding research questions for this portion of the study are: Do members of this group have access to social support networks? How involved are elderly gay men with family, friends, church, and community? Data clearly support the assertion that members of this group are socially engaged. Presumably the level of social engagement indicates that these men either have someone to go to, should they need social support, or they have someone to ask for advice regarding where or to whom to go to for social support. In addition, these men are very involved with friends and community. Although the majority of men indicated having siblings or being out to family, they seem to be more reliant on friends for support. Their involvement with church also varied, with some being active in church organizations or clubs and others not.

HOUSING

Guiding research questions related to housing are: What are the housing needs of the aging gay male community? and, What housing needs are anticipated in the future? Respondents were asked about their current living situation in addition to where they thought they would be living in 5, 10, and 20 years from now and with whom they thought they would be living. Not surprisingly, the responses varied according to age and whether respondents were in relationships.

Table 4.9 illustrates housing characteristics of the respondents. The majority of persons taking part in this research own their dwelling (81.6 percent), and the majority live in traditional, stand-alone housing (70.4 percent). The number of respondents living alone was almost equally divided, with over 51 percent living with someone,

TABLE 4.9. Living Arrangements of Survey Participants

Characteristic/Question	N	Percent
Own or Rent		
Own	102	81.6
Rent	22	17.6
Missing	1	0.8
Type of Dwelling		
House	88	70.4
Condo	17	13.6
Apartment	18	14.4
Other	2	1.6
Cohabitate		
Yes	64	51.2
No	61	48.8
Cohabitator Relationship		
Friend/roommate	5	7.9
Significant other	55	85.9
Wife/heterosexual spouse	2	3.1
Family member	2	3.1
Live in Gay Neighborhood		
Yes	14	1.2
No	95	76.0
Mixed	16	12.8

and almost 49 percent living alone. For persons cohabitating (N = 64), almost 86 percent live with a significant other or partner. Only a small number live with friends (7.9 percent), heterosexual spouses (3.1 percent), or other family members (3.1 percent). The greatest proportion of respondents (76 percent) do not live in a gay neighborhood, even though, as noted earlier, the cities of Dallas and Houston do have clearly defined "gay neighborhoods." San Antonio and Austin do not have such definitive geographic locales.

Responses to research questions about current housing needs and future needs are not what were anticipated. Discussion has been generated within the Dallas gay community about the need for gay-specific housing; however, these data seem to provide little support for this idea. Neither the survey nor the interviews provided the anticipated support for the concept of gay-specific housing for the elderly gay population either currently or in the future. Interestingly, although some men did verbalize the need or desire for gay-specific housing, two observations were noted. The first of these is that respondents do not want to consider living in a place other than their current residence, or if they do move, they want to move to a place of their own choosing. Apparently respondents want to avoid any situation which they perceive as a loss of independence. Living in a structured environment, even if it is the most minimal of assisted living, connotes a sense of loss of control. For example, one respondent, when asked if he would consider living in gay-specific housing for the elderly, said,

> Only if I had to, I guess. I mean if I was, you know, if I didn't have a partner and my partner died, or I became seriously ill, I'd do something like that. But as long as I'm healthy, I'm not going to, you know, it's just for those that . . . I'm sure that's what those are for, is for those that can't afford to live on their own.

Another respondent talked of the idea of integration between homosexual and heterosexual elderly and said,

> I think we're going to see more of an integrated society. I think in the future, I think that there have been great strides made toward acceptance of you know, gays in general. There will always be those people who are bigoted and hateful toward gays because they're ignorant and they don't understand, but basically I think that our lifestyle is generally no different than a heterosexual lifestyle. It seems that we strive for the same things that anyone strives for.

Although some participants did indicate their desire for gay-only housing, many did not due to the fact that they wanted the choice and freedom not to be institutionalized. With regard to the future housing needs of the community, respondents asserted that they thought in the future, gays and lesbians would be more accepted than they are today and that integration into traditional (i.e., heterosexual) housing for the elderly would not be a problem.

Respondents were asked where they thought they would be living in the next 5, 10, and 20 years and if they thought they would be living alone. Furthermore, they were asked, if they did not think they would be living alone, with whom they thought they would be living. Few anticipated a different living situation in five years. However, several said they anticipated a move in ten years. This occurred when a working respondent anticipated retiring in a different locale, or for older persons, many said they thought they would be in an assisted-living facility. Not surprising, those persons who were single anticipated moving into an assisted-living facility, while those who were coupled invariably indicated their housing situation would not change even in 20 years. For the 20-year mark, many said they thought they would be dead and indicated they would be living in a "cemetery," "underground," or "cremated."

During the interviews, participants said that housing needs for aging gays were no different than housing for aging heterosexuals. In fact, one person said, when asked about the perceived housing needs of the aging gay male community, "No different than the entire aging community." When asked in a follow-up probe, "Which is what?" he said, "Well, some of them are going to have to have government-supported housing, and, of course, those [in] assisted-living or nursing homes. For most of them don't have any money." When asked if he meant that a need existed for affordable housing he responded with a resounding, "Yes." Another respondent echoed this sentiment by stating of the current housing needs, "No different than anybody else, I don't think." Again, very little support was voiced for gay-specific housing, although one person did find the idea appealing,

> I think there's a big need. . . . There could be a lot of companionship there, as opposed to moving into a straight assisted-living retirement home or nursing home and have to be completely homophobic there. I can see all the wonderful activities that could be contributed to that and would help the gay men or women to be more happy.

The theme that recurred with regard to housing was affordability. One respondent did live in an independent living facility and talked about its affordability and the fact that he planned to live there until they carried him out "feet first." He also mentioned the "gay corner" of his floor where several residents were either known or presumed to be gay.

HEALTH AND WELL-BEING

Specific research questions regarding health and well-being were: How do aging gay men describe their health and well-being? Do aging gay men consider themselves to be physically healthy? Do members of this population suffer from depression? If they do suffer from depression, what do they perceive as the cause? For explanatory purposes and discussion, two tables are provided, one showing physical health characteristics and one showing mental health attributes.

Physical Health

Table 4.10 illustrates some physical health attributes of survey respondents. The respondent pool was largely made up of those who exercise (68.8 percent) about two to three times per week (46.5 percent); described their physical health as good (56 percent) or excellent (24 percent); take medications regularly (79.2 percent); do not smoke (88.8 percent); do drink alcohol (71.2 percent); and typically drink wine (52.8 percent) and/or liquor (48 percent).

Few of the respondents were regulars at a health club or gym even though they reported regular exercise. The majority who exercised did aerobic/cardiovascular activity which included such things as regular walking or riding a stationary bicycle. Many of the interview respondents talked about aerobic activity in their daily routines. For example, one person said,

Usually if I buy wood, I carry it up the stairs. I walk. In the summertime, I'd say maybe once a week or something, on a nice day. But I do a lot of walking at work.

Another person said,

It's cardio. I had a heart operation two years ago and since then I've been in a cardiac rehab program and subsequently went into a cardiovascular strengthening program at the YMCA. And I do that to maintain my health and to build my strength back up.

One person was very structured with his exercise schedule and said, "I go to the gym. I do thirty minutes of cardiovascular and I do thirty minutes of conditioning." There were no runners in this group and no one did any form of regular or extensive weight training.

Expounding on some of the previous information, the mean number of drinks per week reported was nine. With regard to medication use, the respondents were generally dependent on medication for various ailments, such as hypertension, cholesterol, diabetes, cancer (prostate or other), or depression.

Because the human immunodeficiency virus (HIV) and acquired immunodeficiency syndrome (AIDS) have had such a dramatic impact on the gay community, respondents were asked about their HIV status. Over 80 percent (83.2 percent) of respondents reported having been tested while almost 13 percent stated that they had not been tested (see Table 4.11). The last testing date for those who had been tested ranged from as far back as October 1987 to as recent as March 2001. Of the 104 respondents who had been tested, five (4.8 percent) indicated that they were HIV positive, and over 95 percent said they were HIV negative. When asked if HIV had an impact on their lives, the majority (68.8 percent) of the respondents said that it had. HIV affected these men in various ways; some reported having lost friends, family members, or previous partners to the virus. Those who reported not having been

TABLE 4.10. Physical Health Characteristics of Survey Participants

Characteristic	N	Percent
Exercise		
Yes	86	68.8
No	35	28.0
Missing	4	3.2
Frequency of Exercise		
Once a month	2	2.3
> once a month	3	3.5
2-4 times per month	7	8.1
Once a week	12	14.0
2-3 times per week	40	46.5
> 3 times per week	22	25.6
Description of Physical Health		
Excellent	30	24.0
Good	70	56.0
Fair	19	15.2
Poor	2	1.6
Missing	4	3.2
Regular Medications		
Yes	99	79.2
No	23	18.4
Missing	3	2.4
Smoking Behavior		
Yes	10	8.0
No	111	88.8
Missing	4	3.2
Drinking Behavior		
Yes	89	71.2
No	33	26.4
Missing	3	2.4
Wine Drinking		
Yes	66	52.8
No	24	19.2
Missing	35	28.0
Beer Drinking		
Yes	41	32.8
No	50	40.0
Missing	34	27.2
Liquor Drinking		
Yes	60	48.0
No	30	24.0
Missing	35	28.0

TABLE 4.11. Reported HIV/AIDS Status of Survey Participants

Item	N	Percent
Previously Tested		
Yes	104	83.2
No	16	12.8
Missing	5	4.0
HIV Status		
Positive	5	4.8
Negative	99	95.2
HIV Impact		
Yes	86	68.8
No	36	28.8
Missing	3	2.4

tested for HIV/AIDS, when selected for an interview, were asked why. One person said,

> I just don't want to know. I think I'd be depressed if I . . . I just don't want to know. And my partner doesn't want to be tested either. I just don't want to know. I mean I may have it and I just don't want to know.

Another respondent said,

> I don't know. Fear maybe. I really don't think that I'm HIV positive because I've had safe sex or have kept sex safe for years and years and years and have had no symptoms and it's almost immaterial at this point because the medicine seems to have its side effects. . . .Whatever rationalization you want to use.

In short, these respondents generally described themselves as in good or excellent health even though most were dependent on regular medications. They described engagement in exercise two to three times per week and a lifestyle generally void of cigarette smoking.

Mental Health/Well-Being

Respondents were asked various questions about depression, happiness, and stigma in an effort to get at their self-perceptions of mental health. Responses to these questions are in Table 4.12. In addressing the mental health attributes of respondents, the majority described themselves as very happy (38.4 percent) or fairly happy (42.4 percent). In fact, only about 17 percent described themselves as not very happy, not at all happy, or incapable of choosing a response. When these respondents were asked what

TABLE 4.12. Perceived Mental Well-Being of Survey Participants

Characteristic	N	Percent
Perceived Happiness		
Very happy	48	38.4
Fairly happy	53	42.4
Not very happy	18	14.4
Not at all happy	1	0.8
Can't choose	2	1.6
Missing	3	2.4
Previous Psychological Therapy		
Yes	86	48.0
No	36	50.4
Missing	3	1.6
Current Psychological Therapy		
Yes	6	4.8
No	85	68.0
Missing	34	27.2
Experience Depression		
Yes	31	24.8
No	44	35.2
Sometimes	48	38.4
Missing	2	1.6
Experience Loneliness		
Yes	16	12.8
No	62	49.6
Sometimes	44	35.2
Missing	3	2.4

would make them happier, they indicated such things as having a partner, better health, more money ("winning the lottery"), more friends, more travel, and a (better) job. Some of the less typical responses included one respondent who said that having a size 32 waist would make him happier. When asked if he was doing anything to get to that size he said, "Well, no. If I would exercise I could be there again." Another respondent said a better work environment would make him happier. One person said that less of an emphasis by the gay community on bars and sex would make him happier.

Respondents were asked what makes a man adjust well to growing old and the majority indicated general things such as self-acceptance of age and sexuality, friends, romantic/sexual relationships, meaningful social groups, financial security, and good health. This general idea of self-acceptance is illustrated by the following response:

> Well, I think when one accepts the fact that you are gay, that you're different, that you're considered different by society, you can accept the fact that you are gay and that you live in a—as a minority in a "straight" world. And I find that my association with people is much more congenial and accepting. I have lots of straight people that I've worked with that I live . . . neighbors and that sort of thing, who've accepted me. And I think that's part of just growing old gracefully and accepting your lifestyle and accepting the world that you live in.

Almost one-half of survey respondents (48 percent) reported that they had received some form of counseling or psychological therapy in the past. However, under five percent indicated that they are currently seeing a therapist.

Some research questions focused on the respondents' experiences with depression and the perception of its cause, and their experience with loneliness. The results were very similar. In fact, almost one-fourth (24.8 percent) said they did get depressed, over 38 percent said they did sometimes, and 35 percent said they did not.

Respondents were asked what they perceive the cause of their depression to be and they noted such things as their age/aging, physical decline/health problems, and their financial situations. In addition, almost half (48 percent) reported experiencing loneliness at least some of the time.

Although this research is not made up of randomly selected participants and tests of association were not appropriate, some cross tabulations were run in order to look at possible associations between variables. Tables 4.13, 4.14, and 4.15 show the cross tabulation between relationship status and the variables of happiness, depression, and loneliness.

As illustrated in Table 4.13, it seems that persons in committed relationships perceive themselves as happier than those who are single or casually dating. They also perceive themselves as vastly happier than those who consider themselves in "other" types of relationships.

Table 4.14 shows the cross tabulation of relationship status and perception of depression. Disregarding the "sometimes" category, since most people would probably say they get depressed sometimes, the data indicate that respondents who are in committed relationships perceive themselves as experiencing depression less than those who are in other categories.

Table 4.15 shows the cross tabulations between relationship status and perception of loneliness. Clearly, respondents in this survey who are in committed relationships experience loneliness much less than persons who are single or casually dating. Cer-

TABLE 4.13. Relationship Status and Perceived Happiness of Survey Participants

Happiness	Relationship Status (Percentages)			
	Single	Casually Dating	In a Committed Relationship	Other
Very happy	20.8	16.7	64.2	
Fairly happy	54.7	66.6	28.6	40.0
Not very happy	22.6	16.7	3.6	60.0
Not at all happy			1.8	
Can't choose	1.9		1.8	

TABLE 4.14. Relationship Status and Perceived Depression of Survey Participants

	Relationship Status (Percentages)			
Depression	Single	Casually Dating	In a Committed Relationship	Other
Yes	29.6	50.0	17.9	20.0
No	37.0	16.7	39.3	20.0
Sometimes	33.4	33.3	42.8	60.0

TABLE 4.15. Relationship Status and Perceived Loneliness of Survey Participants

	Relationship Status (Percentages)			
Loneliness	Single	Casually Dating	In a Committed Relationship	Other
Yes	17.0		8.9	40.0
No	32.1	16.7	75.0	20.0
Sometimes	50.9	83.3	16.1	60.0

tainly these three tables suggest the importance of companionship for successful navigation of the aging process.

Table 4.16 includes information associated with the stigma related to aging and homosexuality. Respondents were asked about their experiences with having to pass as heterosexual and if they perceived having experienced stigma associated with either homosexuality or aging. Not surprisingly, over 70 percent (71.2 percent) said that they had previously had to pass as heterosexual. However, when asked about the stigma associated with being homosexual, responses were split down the middle with 48.8 percent indicating they had and 48.8 percent indicating they had not experienced stigma related to being gay. This is surprising since such a large percentage mentioned having to pass as heterosexual. When asked in what way they had experienced stigma, participants elaborated with narratives primarily about job discrimination (i.e., promotions or being denied work), physical harassment, loss of friends, or being shunned by family. One person said,

Going into restaurants with all men and people, straights, looking over. You can't talk. Straights look over; even people who own the restaurant are discriminatory. You go to the theater, people look down on you.

Another person said,

I had a boss who was extremely homophobic. He didn't make any bones about it and he did not like having older people work for him. He only wanted to have employees who were his age or younger. I did not get promoted. I retired before he left the organization.

Over half of the respondents (54.4 percent) said they had not experienced stigma related to aging, while 44 percent said they had. When asked to elaborate, respondents reported experiencing stigma in the work environment, and in being shunned by younger gay men. One other respondent told about a younger group of gay men who scratched his car with a key in the church parking lot after realizing he was an older gay man.

TABLE 4.16. Stigma Perceived by Survey Participants

Stigma	N	Percent
Having to Pass As Heterosexual		
Yes	89	71.2
No	32	25.6
Missing	4	3.2
Gay Stigma Experience		
Yes	61	48.8
No	61	48.8
Missing	3	2.4
Aging Stigma Experience		
Yes	55	44.0
No	68	54.4
Missing	2	1.6

To conclude the survey, respondents were asked questions related to employment, and about things left on a "to-do" list, what their top three concerns are as they age, what they would like the government to do for aging gays, and about regrets. These data are presented in Table 4.18.

EMPLOYMENT CHARACTERISTICS

The respondents' employment status ranged from retired to full-time employment, with most (52.8 percent) self-identifying as retired. Over one-third of survey respondents (33.6 percent) indicated that they were employed full-time in occupations ranging from airline reservationist and file clerk to college professor and physician. Fifty-two respondents gave information regarding their income, which ranged from $0 to over $90,000. The median income category for this group was $45,001 to $60,00. Over one-fourth (26.4 percent) of those responding to a question about retirement said they had plans for retirement, while almost 17 percent said they did not. When asked if they were looking forward to retirement, 24 percent said they were, while 16 percent said they were not. Those who were retired were asked to report the amount of their last annual income before taxes. The median income category was $30,001 to $45,000. Table 4.17 shows these data.

Interviewees were asked about their notions of retirement. Not surprisingly, respondents said they thought they would feel useless or not needed and that they could not imagine not having anything to do or anyplace to be. For these men, retirement meant a loss of connectedness to a world in which they felt useful. They asserted that work was purposeful. In fact, one person who had retired and gone back to work full-time talked about his experience:

> I love to work. And that period of time when I was retired, I felt awful. I felt not needed. Not wanted. Nobody wanted me. I applied for job after job, no interviews. When I left my age and my salary off of the applications the telephone rang off the wall.

TABLE 4.17. Employment Characteristics of Survey Participants

Item	N	Percent
Employment Status		
Employed, full-time	42	33.6
Employed, < full-time	9	7.2
Unemployed/disability	2	1.6
Unemployed	1	0.8
Retired	66	52.8
Other	1	0.8
Missing	4	3.2
Employed Income Before Taxes		
$0-15,000	1	0.8
$15,001-30,000	8	6.4
$30,001-45,000	14	11.2
$45,001-60,000	10	8.0
$60,001-75,000	6	4.8
$75,001-90,000	9	7.2
$90,001+	3	2.4
Don't know	1	0.8
Missing	73	58.4
Retirement Plans		
Yes	33	26.4
No	21	16.8
Looking Forward to Retiring		
Yes	30	24.0
No	20	16.0
Retired, Last Income Before Taxes		
$0-15,000	1	0.8
$15,001-30,000	16	12.8
$30,001-45,000	18	14.4
$45,001-60,000	14	11.2
$60,001-75,000	13	10.4
$75,001-90,000	2	1.6
$90,001+	4	3.2
Missing	57	45.6

Another respondent said,

> Waking up in the morning with nothing to do is not what I want to do. Now the time may come—the time may come when I wake up in the morning and my goal in life is to keep the house clean; do the remodeling, which I've been planning since the last century, a little bit of travel, but at the moment, I just like to have a more, a bigger chunk of life to chew, if you will.

These were typical responses of persons not looking forward to retiring.

SOME CLOSING THOUGHTS

Concluding the survey was a section in which participants were asked (in an open-ended question) to indicate whether they had things they still wanted to do. The question yielded interesting results because the majority (68.8 percent) said that they did have things they were still interested in doing. Most of the responses related to travel, either more or to specific destinations such as Europe, Australia, or various parts of the United States, such as the East or the West. A few said they were interested in finding a significant other. One person said he wanted to finish a novel he had been working on for several years; another said he wanted to go sledding in Vermont; still another said that there were sexual activities he had yet to experience.

Respondents were also asked about regrets and if there was one thing they could change about the way their lives have gone, what it would be. Interestingly, the majority (65.6 percent) of respondents said they did not have any regrets about the way their lives had turned out. For those that said they did have regrets (34.4 percent), some of the things mentioned were that they regretted not coming out at an earlier age; they regretted such things as not trying hard enough to find a partner or not saving enough money. One person said he regretted being gay:

You bet. It'd be a hell of a lot better to be in this life being straight. . . . getting married, having kids, grandkids, and retire. Being accepted in the community. Being accepted in the church . . .

Some talked about bad career choices as things they would change and others named issues such as coming out to particular family members (mainly parents), or coming out earlier in life. Several respondents said they would have acquired more education, exited or entered relationships sooner, or they would have had children. Table 4.18 shows the frequencies things left on "to-do" lists and persons mentioning life regrets.

Respondents were asked what, if anything, they would like the government to do for aging gays. Many responses were gay-specific, such as "Treat us like everyone else," meaning benefits of heterosexual persons (rights of survivorship, for example), or "Pass human rights laws." Other responses were more age-related such as "Provide health coverage," "Low-cost medications," and "Affordable housing." One respondent did say, "Leave us alone." When I asked him during an interview what he meant by that response, he verbalized feelings regarding too much government intervention in the lives of American citizens.

I was curious about whether the Internet has created a situation whereby persons would perhaps have one more avenue for social connectivity, so I asked interview respondents only about whether the Internet has impacted their lives. A few said that it had no effect,

TABLE 4.18. Concluding Remarks of Survey Participants

Item	N	Percent
Things Left to Do		
Yes	86	68.8
No	36	28.8
Missing	3	2.4
Life Regrets		
Yes	43	34.4
No	82	65.6

since they had no computer or no Internet access from home; however, many said it had (1) increased their access to information; (2) provided a quicker, more convenient means for communication; and (3) provided an opportunity for dating situations to be created. For example, one person said,

> It's very interesting to me and I am absolutely amazed about the information that is there on the Internet under any subject—anything that you want to look up. It's, you know—it's like having your own personal library. You can look up anything you want to. And [it] just boggles my mind that it's there. It's available. I cannot conceive, now that I've gotten into the Internet, why more people aren't more into it. Because of the relatively inexpensive equipment to get there and what is available to them from the Internet.

Another respondent said,

> A great deal. I would say two ways. First of all, my work is involved in the Internet because the cables that we're putting up now will be carrying Internet traffic, so the cable companies hope. Second of all, it is something that I use almost on a daily basis to gather information or to send information.

A third respondent said,

> I've bought a lot of stuff on eBay. You could certainly get knowledge off the Internet faster. I'm into stocks and I check them quite often on the computer. You can, you know, there's some things that you want knowledge and you go to the computer. I think the Internet is great. I don't know whether it's changed my life or not, but I guess anything you do changes it, but I've never considered it something that has changed my life.

Survey respondents were also asked about the best and the worst aspects of aging. For the best aspects of aging, some of the typical responses given were things such as wisdom, discounts, respect, financial independence/financial security, retirement, and freedom from the time constraints of work or other responsibilities. Some respondents saw no positive aspects of aging. For example, an interview respondent who said, "None" on his survey, when asked to elaborate replied, "I can't think a [positive] thing about it. I think everything about aging is bad. I can't think of a thing." For questions related to the worst aspects of aging, the typical response was related to physical health. Decreased mobility or poor health were frequent responses, as were "aches and pains" and not having enough money. For example, one respondent said not having energy. This was related to physical health problems. Another respondent said, "Sagging skin."

SUMMARY

In analyzing the research questions guiding this study, the housing needs of the aging gay male community seem a bit unclear. Participants indicated that housing is needed, yet they do not see themselves leaving their residence of choice. Moving into a housing facility, including a gay-only facility, is apparently viewed as a loss of independence. Moreover, many said that they presumed homosexuals will become more socially integrated and be able to live among homosexuals in an assisted-living situation without homophobia or heterosexism. The gay men in this study described themselves as healthy or in good health, and not generally somewhat depressed. Those who described themselves as depressed perceive the reasons to be related to such things as their health, being single, financial worries, or loneliness. Access to social support networks are apparently perceived as readily available. This is not surprising as respondents were primarily either churchgoers or members of the Prime Timers Worldwide organization. Finally, respondents did indicate a connection to family and friends, church, and the community at large.

Chapter 5

Discussion and Conclusion

This study was exploratory in nature. Survey research was conducted with 125 men in four Texas cities: Austin, Dallas, Houston, and San Antonio. In addition, in-depth interviews were carried out with 20 gay men in Dallas. Although this was a small-scale study, data have been provided on how aging gay men define and perceive their experiences of aging. Generally speaking, those who took part in this study were white-collar workers, educated, socially engaged, happy, and in good physical health. These characteristics are not surprising. Existing research documents the fact that a select group of people is typically included in studies such as this (see Berger 1996).

For the purposes of presentation and explanation, this chapter is structured in the same manner as the previous chapters so that the study is summarized topically, and relevant findings and conclusions grouped accordingly.

SOCIAL SUPPORT/RELATIONSHIPS/INVOLVEMENT

Research questions related to social support were geared toward an understanding of whether aging gay men remain engaged and have access to social support should they need it. Most persons said they did, in fact, have direct access to social support networks. When a respondent did not have firsthand knowledge of an agency name or phone number, he was aware of a friend or person to call for this type of information. The second research question sought to explore, again, whether aging gay men remain engaged in/with their families, social activities, church, and the community. These men were engaged, which was not surprising, given the sources of the sample. Respondents were primarily recruited through a social organization for gay men, gay churches, and friendship circles.

The literature related to aging gay males is replete with stereotypes of gay men who are single, lonely, depressed, and uninvolved in the social world (Kimmel 1978; Berger 1996). However, the studies conducted by Kimmel and Berger challenge these misconceptions, and the present study does the same thing. The men in this research were very socially engaged and involved, either with organized activities, with friendship networks, or with a significant other. This is also true of respondents in previous research studies (Berger 1996; Slusher et al. 1996). However, it is possible that methodological restrictions with this kind of research bias the findings in that researchers are more likely to be able to locate and to interview/survey those who are socially engaged. It is difficult to study those whose sexual orientation is a well-kept secret or to study those who are not engaged in social circles or networks. Certainly this is an issue that should be dealt with methodologically and reconciled, as previous researchers have made this same observation (see Slusher et al. 1996).

HOUSING

This research did little to clarify the housing needs of the aging gay community. Although rhetoric has been generated about a "need," this study fails to provide support for such an assertion (see Lucco 1987; McDonald 1998; Devlin 2000). Few men, during the interviews, mentioned housing as a need or concern. Those who did acknowledge housing for the elderly to be a viable need for the gay community were, in most cases, unwilling to live in such facilities. The respondents perceived institutional housing as serving those who are indigent, infirm, single, and/or incapable of self-care. Respondents viewed institutional living as a "last resort" (see Fokkema and Van Wissen 1997). With regard to gay-specific housing for the future, some asserted that they thought U.S. society would continue to be more integrated regarding sexual orientation, so that gay-specific housing would not be needed. Generally, respondents did agree that the number of aging gays is growing as life expectancies increase and as persons continue to disclose their homosexuality and begin to lead openly gay lives. However, with regard to housing, the recurring theme was affordability rather than homosexual exclusivity. Although housing for the homosexual community was not given high priority by the respondents in this research, interest in building nationwide housing and retirement communities exist, if not exclusively for gays and lesbians, at least for those that will be "gay friendly."

HEALTH AND WELL-BEING

Mental/Psychological Health

This study sought to understand whether aging gay males considered themselves to be depressed and, if so, what they considered to be the cause. Only about one-fourth of respondents reported themselves as depressed while another 38 percent said that they were "sometimes." Putting aside those who said they were "sometimes depressed," because most persons would probably say this if they are honest, this leaves about one-fourth for whom depression may be a problem. Cross tabulation of relationship status with reported depression suggested that there might be an association since only about 18 percent of those in committed relationships were depressed. In open-ended questions on the survey, respondents noted reasons for depression as aches and pains, financial woes, aging, and being single. Berger (1984) and Lipman (1986) assert the importance for gay men to be with others who are like them. Their findings suggest that respondents in this research would not experience high rates of depression because they are largely involved and socially networked.

Woodman (1989) and Adelman (1991) mention the importance of loss for aging gays and successfully coping with it. Respondents in this study dealt with loss of friends, family, and loved ones due to natural aging-related deaths, but also those deaths related to HIV/AIDS. This became apparent when a majority of the men surveyed reported that HIV/AIDS had impacted their lives. The loss of a significant other is also an important issue as it relates to the psychological health of aging gay men. One respondent self-identified as a "widow." During the interview it was clarified that he considered himself widowed from his same-sex partner who had died in an accident. The interviewee was very upset about this loss, which had transpired about six months prior, and indicated the importance of bereavement support.

Also related to psychological health, the importance of social support is apparent. Because these men were actively engaged in Prime Timers, a gay church, or a friendship network, they did have access to social support. It should be noted that although Prime Timers seems to be primarily a social organization, it could be assumed that an informal social support system is created in social situations by virtue of enabling friendships and acquaintanceships. For example, participants in the Slusher et al. (1996) study utilized as their social support organization Gays and Lesbians Older and Wiser (GLOW). For respondents in this study, Prime Timers and the Austin and Dallas churches presumably filled that social support role. It is also clear that the respondents had made use of mental health clinicians, in that 48 percent reported having been in psychological counseling at some point in their past. Respondents were not asked why they were in counseling; however, only 5 percent reported currently being in therapy, suggesting its past use for maintenance of mental health and/or prevention of dysfunctional (relationship or marital) problems. According to the Federal Interagency Forum on Aging-Related Statistics, severe depression rates for elderly men are as follows: for the age group of 65 to 69, depression rates are 9.10 percent; 70 to 74, 9.96 percent; 75 to 79, 10.51 percent 80 to 84, 15.61 percent; and for men age 85 and older the rate of depression is 16.31 percent. Data are not available on what portion of the U.S. population has utilized mental health services in their lifetime. However, the 5 percent currently in therapy in this study is below the 15 percent annual rate for adults in the nation as a whole.

Physical Health

The majority of respondents in this research did describe their health and well-being in positive ways and considered themselves to be in "excellent" or "good" health. This group of respondents was composed of largely nonsmokers and those who regularly exercise. However, participants involved in this research were largely medication dependent for such conditions as hypertension, cancer (prostate), diabetes, elevated cholesterol, arthritis, asthma, HIV, and thyroid problems. The literature related to gays and health care indicates that disclosure of sexual orientation can be an issue in receiving adequate health care. This study did not explore issues of patient or physician disclosure, but presumably, because participants were being treated for various ailments, they were being adequately cared for regardless of their homosexuality or disclosure of their sexual orientation. The AMA has dealt with the stigma associated with being homosexual and asserts that physicians need to obtain a medical history in a nonjudgmental manner. Recently, the GLMA wrote a companion document to the Healthy People 2010 initiative to specifically outline the needs of the gay/lesbian/bisexual/transgender communities. The document calls for specific treatments and considerations for persons in this population.

Most respondents in this study were reportedly HIV negative. However, the literature indicates that HIV/AIDS is an issue for the aging community. Generally, aging persons are not targeted for prevention education initiatives due to the misconceptions that they are not sexually active or engaged in intravenous drug use (Emlet 1997). HIV/AIDS affects every age category. People who are 55 and older are contracting HIV, developing AIDS, and dying. The CDC reports that almost 6 percent of the cumulative AIDS cases reported involve persons aged 55 and older (Centers for Disease Control 2001a). Of the cumulative number of AIDS deaths, almost 8 percent are men aged 55 and older (Centers for Disease Control 2001b). This group of people needs to be targeted for HIV prevention education and tested when presented in a medical setting. Although most respondents were HIV negative, they nevertheless felt the impact of the virus in various ways.

THEMATIC FINDINGS
AND THEORETICAL IMPLICATIONS

Several authors note the manner in which one can accomplish a "successful" aging process. For example, Friend (1991) asserts the need for one to accept his or her homosexuality as part of the successful aging process. In fact, Friend has come up with a conceptual model whereby persons fit into one of three identities: stereotypical older homosexual, passing older homosexual, or affirmative older homosexual. He asserts that regardless of which of the three identities one assumes, the importance lies in self-acceptance. This idea of "self-acceptance" was a theme that emerged from the data (see also Berger 1984). In fact, this idea of self-acceptance was generated when participants spoke of "growing old gracefully." One interview respondent stated that growing old gracefully had to do with self-acceptance as a homosexual and as a member of a certain age group. Thus, the need to accept not only one's age but also one's homosexuality is a way to successfully navigate the aging process. Berger (1984) addresses the notion of successful aging as well and mentions the importance of accepting oneself in a larger social context (see also Minnigerode and Adelman 1978).

The grounded theory approach was utilized in this study to allow patterns of responses emerging from the data to take their own meaning rather than being contextualized by hypotheses or preconceived theories. Themes that have been previously mentioned emerged from the data. The theme of affordable but preferably not institutionalized housing was one that several respondents voiced. Successful aging was another theme that emerged as respondents talked about acceptance of themselves and of the world around them.

Although the utilization of grounded theory was the goal of this research, no new theory was generated. If this study does anything to create or promote new theory, it at least serves to negate misconceptions of older gay men as lonely, depressed social deviants. Indeed, another theme to emerge from these data is how these aging gay males are like all other people in what they want and need.

A few of the men did perceive stigma. For example, one respondent talked about his perceptions of public and heterosexist settings such as restaurants and theaters. However, most of the men did not perceive themselves as having experienced much stigma related to being gay. This is interesting, since the literature asserts that aging gay men experience stigma and that effective stigma management is one way to achieve successful aging (Kimmel 1978; Friend 1991). Sociologically speaking, and using Goffman's (1963) concept of "impression management," the fact that men in this study did not seem to perceive being stigmatized is related to social class. Some of the participants were clearly skilled in impression management perhaps practiced over the years to the point that such management is now a subconscious way of life. Most participants in this study also possessed the resources (such as education, income, and occupation) to enable and support such management. Because participants in this study were generally white-collar professionals, it was evident, as illustrated by an interview with a pharmacist, for example, that persons in professional occupations do not divulge personal/sexual information regardless of the setting. Professionalism is maintained at all times. During this interview the respondent talked about "everybody knowing" so that "it was not an issue." In having one's homosexuality "not be an issue" one will presumably be exempt from experiencing stigma associated with a "spoiled identity" (Goffman 1963). Again, for the middle-class gay man, this means that avoidance of sex talk at work serves the white-collar homosexual as a means to avoid reiterating or divulging a stigmatizing identity. Having "everybody know" without needing to mention it repeatedly enables the gay man to fit in based on occupation, social class, and professional status, rather than keeping him on the fringes of society based on sexual orientation.

STUDY LIMITATIONS

This study had several limitations. The first and most important is sampling. Participants for this study were solicited via a social organization composed of aging gay men. In addition, persons were recruited via a gay/lesbian church and several friendship networks. This snowball and convenience methodology did not allow for random sampling and, consequently, participants in this study are not representative of aging gay men in general. This methodology also restricted the recruitment of persons to those who were socially engaged in one aspect or another and also biased the research toward white and middle-class respondents. Another limitation related to sampling is size. To get a better understanding of aging gay men in Texas, perhaps more surveys and interviews could have been utilized (particularly in different settings) in order to allow for the possibility of a more diverse sample.

FUTURE RESEARCH

Suggestions for future research include a more representative sample and reiterating the views of other researchers for the need to examine persons who are on the "fringes" of social engagement (Slusher et al. 1996). It should be determined whether a more representative sample will perhaps uncover respondents who are less socially engaged and more like the negative stereotypes (see Kelly 1977; Kimmel 1978; Berger 1996). The study of gay men in other parts of the United States will provide more general information on the experience of aging gay men and perhaps add to the ethnic and racial mix of research respondents. Finally, revisiting the field at a future date will provide data on whether, in fact, aging gays do become more socially integrated into their largely heterosexual age cohorts, as some respondents in this study have predicted. It will also be interesting to learn how social services, housing, and health needs will be met as the number of aging gays continues to increase.

SUMMARY

A call for further research with more diverse samples is in order. As the U.S. population continues to age and live longer, and as homosexuals continue to disclose their sexuality or live as openly gay and lesbian persons, knowledge and understanding of this population is important. Moreover, it is imperative that social scientists continue to research the homosexual population to gain a better and more complete understanding of the issues confronting this segment of the population, including those affecting aging gay men.

Respondents taking part in this research project were asked what they wanted the government to do for aging gays. Some responses were gay specific, such as "treat us like everyone else [i.e., heterosexuals]," "human rights," "same-sex benefits," as well as those related to an aging population, e.g., affordable health care, coverage for medication costs, and affordable housing.

This work has added to the overall understanding of aging gay males. However, more research is needed for purposes of social policy, service delivery, and public tolerance. Aging gay men are part of our past and future as homosexuals, as men, and as citizens. Ageist and homophobic/heterosexist attitudes generated toward this population serve to isolate a group that does not want or need to be isolated. Furthermore, if the existing gerontology literature presents these elderly people as becoming socially disengaged, it is misrepresenting; and if this population does become isolated and disengaged from friends or family, it seems apparent that these men will do so only against their will.

Appendix A

Respondent Characteristics
by City (Percentages)

Characteristic	Austin	Dallas	Houston	San Antonio
Age				
Range	55-84 years	5-81 years	5-78 years	55-81 years
Median	67.0 years	62.0 years	65.5 years	66.2 years
Mean	67.0 years	63.1 years	65.3 years	64.0 years
Race/Ethnicity				
White	91.42	95.91	92.85	88.46
Latino			7.14	11.54
American Indian	2.85			
African American		4.09		
Other	5.73			
Sexual Orientation				
Homosexual/gay	85.71	100	92.85	85.18
Bisexual	11.42			14.82
Missing	2.87		7.15	
Educational Level				
High school	5.88	12.24	7.70	18.52
Some college	20.59	20.42	15.38	
BS	14.71	32.65	46.15	29.63
MS	35.29	22.45	30.77	33.33
PhD	23.53	12.24		18.52
Heterosexual Marriage				
Yes	54.29	32.65	35.71	18.52
No	45.71	67.35	64.29	81.48
Children				
Yes	40.00	28.57	21.43	18.53
No	60.00	67.35	78.57	77.77
Missing		4.08		3.70

Appendix B
Research Instruments

THE SOCIOLOGY OF AGING: QUESTIONNAIRE

For all of these questions, please place a check mark in the box of the most appropriate response.

Social Support/Relationships/Involvement

1. What is your relationship status?

   ❑ Single
   ❑ Casually dating someone
   ❑ In a committed relationship
   ❑ Other _____

2. For how long?_____

3. If you are in a committed long-term relationship do you have a "marriage" contract or other legal documentation binding you and your partner together?

   ❑ Yes
   ❑ No

4. If single, do you date?

   ❑ Yes
   ❑ No

5. If so, how often?

   ❑ Never
   ❑ Once a year
   ❑ Once a month
   ❑ Once a week
   ❑ More often than once a week
   ❑ Other _____

6. Have you had any difficulty meeting others in your age group for friends, dates?

   ❑ Yes
   ❑ No

7. Would you say your circle of friends is comprised of:

   ❑   Mostly gays
   ❑   Mostly heterosexual people
   ❑   An equal mix of both

8. Do you have brothers and sisters?

   ❑ Yes
   ❑ No

9. Generally, would you say you have a close relationship with brothers and sisters?

   ❑ Yes
   ❑ No
   ❑ With some (or one) but not all

10. Have you ever been involved in a heterosexual marriage?

   ❑ Yes
   ❑ No

11. If so, how long did that last? _____

12. Do you have children?

   ❑ Yes
   ❑ No

13. If yes, how many? _____

14. If yes, what are their ages? _____

15. Generally speaking, do your friends tend to be older or younger than you?

   ❑ Older
   ❑ Younger
   ❑ Mix of both

16. Are you out to your family?

    ❏ Yes
    ❏ No
    ❏ Out to some

17. Are you out to your friends?

    ❏ Yes
    ❏ No
    ❏ Out to some

18. Are you out to your co-workers?

    ❏ Yes
    ❏ No
    ❏ Out to some

19. Would you say you have a surrogate family of friends who replace blood relatives?

    ❏ Yes
    ❏ No

20. Have you lost the support of any persons to whom you have disclosed your homosexuality?

    ❏ Yes
    ❏ No

21. Do you attend church?

    ❏ Yes
    ❏ No

22. If you do attend church, would you say your attendance is:

    ❏ Regular (3-5 times a month)
    ❏ Irregular (less than 3-5 times per month)

23. What is your religious preference?

    ❏ Protestant
    ❏ Catholic
    ❏ Jewish
    ❏ None
    ❏ Don't know
    ❏ Other _____

24. Would you call yourself a strong (Protestant, Catholic, Jew, Other) or not?

    ❑   Strong
    ❑   Not very strong
    ❑   Somewhat strong
    ❑   No religion
    ❑   Don't know
    ❑   N/A

25. Are you active in any social groups or organizations?

    ❑   Yes
    ❑   No

26. If so, please list all the organizations

    _____
    _____
    _____

27. Would you say your participation is:

    ❑   Very active
    ❑   Moderately active
    ❑   Not very active
    ❑   Other:_____

Housing

1. Do you currently own or rent? _____

2. Do you live in a:

    ❑   House
    ❑   Condominium
    ❑   Apartment
    ❑   Other

3. Do you cohabitate?

    ❑   Yes
    ❑   No

4. If yes, do you live with a:

   ❑ Friend/roommate
   ❑ Significant other/partner
   ❑ Wife/heterosexual spouse
   ❑ Family member
   ❑ Other _____

5. In number of years, how long have you lived in this apartment/house?

   _____

6. Would you say you live in a gay neighborhood?

   ❑ Yes
   ❑ No
   ❑ Mixed

For the next twelve questions related to housing, if you see yourself living in a physical setting other than the one in which you presently reside, please indicate that in the space provided. Some possibilities may be: move in with someone, assisted-living facility, total care facility, hospice, etc.

7. With regard to type of housing, where do you see yourself living in five years?

   ❑ Same place
   ❑ Other

8. If other, where? _____

9. Do you think you will be living alone?

   ❑ Yes
   ❑ No

10. If no, with whom do you think you will be living? _____

11. With regard to type of housing, where do you see yourself living in ten years?

    ❑ Same place
    ❑ Other

12. If other, where? _____

13. Do you think you will be living alone?

   ❑ Yes
   ❑ No

14. If no, with whom do you think you will be living? _____

15. Where do you see yourself living in 20 years?

   ❑ Same place
   ❑ Other

16. If other, where? _____

17. Do you think you will be living alone?

   ❑ Yes
   ❑ No

18. If no, with whom do you think you will be living? _____

Health and Well-Being

1. Have you been tested for HIV?

   ❑ Yes
   ❑ No

2. If so, when was your last HIV test? (month)_____ (year) _____

3. If so, what were the results?

   ❑ Positive
   ❑ Negative

4. Do you exercise?

   ❑ Yes
   ❑ No

5. If so, how often?

   ❑ Less than once a month
   ❑ Once a month
   ❑ 2-4 times a month
   ❑ Once a week
   ❑ 2-3 times a week
   ❑ More often than 2-3 times per week

6. Would you say your physical health is:

   ❑ Excellent
   ❑ Good
   ❑ Fair
   ❑ Poor

7. Do you take any medications regularly?

   ❑ Yes
   ❑ No

8. If so, what for? _____

9. Do you smoke?

   ❑ Yes
   ❑ No

10. If you do smoke, how many cigarettes per day? _____

11. Do you drink alcohol?

    ❑ Yes
    ❑ No

12. If you do drink alcohol, approximately how many drinks per week?

    _____

13. If you do drink alcohol, which do you drink? *(Please check all that apply)*

    ❑ Wine
    ❑ Beer
    ❑ Liquor

14. If you do drink alcohol, do you sometimes drink more than you think you should?

    ❑ Yes
    ❑ No
    ❑ Don't know

15. If you were to consider your life in general these days, how happy or unhappy would you say you are on the whole?

    ❑ Very happy
    ❑ Fairly happy

❑   Not very happy
❑   Not at all happy
❑   Can't choose
❑   No answer

16. What, if anything, would make you happier?

_____

_____

_____

17. What makes a gay man adjust well to growing old?

_____

_____

_____

18. Has HIV impacted your life (such as with circle of friends, family, etc.)?

❑   Yes
❑   No

19. If yes, how?_____

20. Have you ever received psychological therapy?

❑   Yes
❑   No

21. If so, are you receiving it now?

❑   Yes
❑   No

22. Have you had experiences with work or family or friends in which you had to try to pass as heterosexual?

❑   Yes
❑   No

23. Do you perceive that you have had experiences associated with the stigma of being gay?

❑   Yes
❑   No

24. If so, how?

_____

_____

_____

25. Do you perceive that you have experienced stigma associated with aging?

❑   Yes
❑   No

26. If so, how?

_____

_____

_____

27. Do you ever get depressed?

❑   Yes
❑   No
❑   Sometimes

28. If so, about what?

_____

_____

_____

29. If so, how do you cope?

_____

_____

_____

30. Are you lonely?

❑   Yes
❑   No
❑   Sometimes

31. What are some of the best aspects of aging?

    _____

    _____

    _____

32. What are some of the worst aspects of aging?

    _____

    _____

    _____

Employment Status

1. What is your employment status? *(If retired, skip the next five questions.)*

    ❑   Employed, full-time
    ❑   Homemaker/caregiver, full-time
    ❑   Employed less than full-time
    ❑   Unemployed, on disability
    ❑   Unemployed
    ❑   Never employed
    ❑   Retired
    ❑   Other: _____

2. If employed, what do you do? (occupation or job description, *not* employer)

    _____

3. If employed, what is your annual income before taxes?

    ❑ $0-15,000
    ❑ $15,001-30,000
    ❑ $30,001-45,000
    ❑ $45,001-60,000
    ❑ $60,001-75,000
    ❑ $75,001-90,000
    ❑ $90,001+
    ❑   Don't know

4. If employed, what year do you think you will retire? _____

5. If employed, do you have plans for retirement?

   ❑ Yes
   ❑ No

6. If employed, are you looking forward to retiring?

   ❑ Yes
   ❑ No

7. *If retired,* how do you describe your last full-time job? (occupation or job description, *not* employer) _____

8. *If retired,* what was your annual income before taxes during the last year that you were employed? What year was that? _____

   ❑ $0-15,000
   ❑ $15,001-30,000
   ❑ $30,001-45,000
   ❑ $45,001-60,000
   ❑ $60,001-75,000
   ❑ $75,001-90,000
   ❑ $90,001+
   ❑ Don't know

Conclusion

1. What are your top three concerns as an aging male?

   _____

   _____

   _____

2. What are your top three concerns as an aging gay male?

   _____

   _____

   _____

3. What, if anything, would you like to see city, state, or national government do for aging gays?

_____

_____

_____

4. As you age, is there anything on your "to-do" list that you have not yet done?

   ❑ Yes
   ❑ No

5. If yes, what?

_____

_____

_____

6. Do you have any regrets about the way your life has turned out?

   ❑ Yes
   ❑ No

7. If yes, what?

_____

_____

_____

8. If you could change one thing about the way your life has gone what would it be?

_____

_____

_____

Demographics

   1. What is your age? _____

   2. What is your gender identity?

      ❑ Male

❑ Female
❑ Transgendered

3. What is your racial/ethnic identity?

❑ African American/black
❑ White/Caucasian/European American
❑ Latin/Hispanic/Mexican American/Puerto Rican/Cuban/South American
❑ Asian/Pacific Islander
❑ American Indian/Native American/Eskimo
❑ Other (please specify): _____

4. Where did you grow up?

City: _____

State: _____

5. In which of the following do you live, or which city do you live closest to?

❑ Dallas/Fort Worth
❑ Austin
❑ Houston
❑ San Antonio

6. What is your zip code? _____

7. Are you a member of Prime Timers of Texas?

❑ Yes
❑ No

8. What is the highest level of education you have attained?

❑ Less than high school
❑ High school
❑ Some college/associate's degree
❑ Bachelor's college degree
❑ Master's college degree
❑ PhD/professional (MD, JD, DDS, etc.)
❑ Other: _____

9. Do you consider yourself:

❏ Homosexual/gay
❏ Bisexual
❏ Heterosexual
❏ Other:_____

10. Is your partner returning a survey also?

❏ Yes
❏ No

11. If so, what is his survey ID number? _____

Thanks very much for your time. If you are willing to sit for an in-depth interview (lasting approximately an hour to an hour and a half) please provide your name and contact information, along with best times to call. *Note that I may be unable to interview all who volunteer due to time and budget constraints.*

Name: _____

Telephone number/e-mail: _____

Best times/days: _____

AGING GAY MALE INTERVIEW GUIDE (1-028)

Social Support/Relationships/Involvement

- Prior to this eight-year relationship, what was your relationship history? At what age did you actively pursue relationships with men? What was dating (availability) like? Did you date older or younger? Why?
- What are the sorts of legal documents that you and your partner have signed?
- You said you have experienced difficulty meeting others for friends/ dates. Why do you think this is so? Where do you meet people (or did you)?
- Socially, do you feel involved and fulfilled or do you feel alone?
- Tell me about the relationship with siblings? You indicated closeness with some but not all. Why is that?
- Why are you out to only some co-workers?
- You have regular church attendance. Do you attend Cathedral of Hope?
- Not active in any church organizations?
- What is OLTA; OLITA?

Housing

- Currently, what do you perceive the housing needs of the aging gay male community to be?
- What do you think the housing needs will be in the future? What do you think about gay/lesbian retirement homes? Do we need one in Dallas? Would you live in one?

Physical and Mental Health

- With regard to exercise, you said you do it two to four times a week. Do you do cardio or weights? Do you work out at a gym?
- If you were to need social support in the Dallas area, either related to being gay, or your age, or your gender, are you aware of services that are available to you?
- Do you have a large circle of friends?
- Would you say you are very social or somewhat shy?

- You indicate that assurance retirement will be financially secure would make you happier. Can you tell me about that response? Is there some reason you doubt that?
- You mentioned that comfort and security of maturity eventually become more important than physical beauty of youth and helps individuals to adjust well to being old. Have you reached this point? What are your perceptions of the importance on physical beauty?
- For what reason did you receive psychological therapy?
- Tell me about sometimes getting depressed about decreasing sexual drive. Is a sexual drive something you want to maintain? Is it a decrease in ability or interest (drive)?
- Some of the worst aspects of the stigma of being old include being seen as less valued and less capable. Do you feel that now?

Employment

- What are your plans for retirement?
- Why are you looking forward to retiring?

Conclusion

- Among your top three concerns as an aging male is a decreasing sexual drive. Why is this a concern?
- Is there anything left on your "to-do" list?
- Your life change would have been to have older gay role models. Knowing this, are you trying to be a role model to younger gays?
- How has the Internet affected your life?
- Can you describe a typical week?

AGING GAY MALE INTERVIEW GUIDE (1-045)

Social Support/Relationships/Involvement

- You say you are single. How long have you been single? Why don't you date? What is the pool of available people like? What is the age range of persons you are interested in for dating? Younger? Older? Why?
- You said you have experienced difficulty meeting others for friends/dates. Why do you think this occurs?
- When were you married for five years? Was homosexuality the reason for divorce?
- Socially, do you feel involved and fulfilled or do you feel alone?

Housing

- On your survey, you indicated that you thought you would be living in Dallas or Tulsa in five years. What's in Tulsa? Why do you think you will be living alone? No hope for partner?
- Currently, what do you perceive the housing needs of the aging gay male community to be?
- What do you think the housing needs will be in the future? What do you think about gay/lesbian retirement homes? Do we need one in Dallas? Would you live in one?

Physical and Mental Health

- With regard to exercise, you said you do that two to three times a week. Do you do cardio or weights? Do you work out at a gym?
- If you were to need social support in the Dallas area, either related to being gay, or your age, or your gender, are you aware of services that are available to you?
- Do you have a large circle of friends?
- Would you say you are very social or somewhat shy?
- You mention sometimes drinking more than you think you should. Do you go out to bars or do you drink at home?
- You say a job with a friendlier environment would make you happier. Where do you work? What is that like? Is it antigay?
- Why did you receive psychological therapy? Was it helpful? When was this?

- You talk about dealing with stigma associated to being gay and having experienced discrimination. Can you tell me about this?
- Tell me about younger gays not being friendly with older gays. In what types of situations?
- You answered "none" with regard to one of the best aspects of aging. Why is this?
- You said one of the worst aspects of aging was older guys wanting younger guys for sex. Does this make you feel left out of the available dating/sex pool?

Employment

- You mentioned having plans for retirement. What are these?
- Why are you not looking forward to retiring?

Conclusion

- What are your top three concerns as an aging male?
- You talk about certain sexual activities being left on your "to-do" list. What are these?
- Your regret was being gay. Why?
- How long have you lived in Dallas?
- Can you describe a typical week?

References

Adelman, Marcy. 1991. "Stigma, Gay Lifestyles, and Adjustment to Aging: A Study of Later-Life Gay Men and Lesbians." *Journal of Homosexuality* 20:7-32.

American Medical Association Council on Scientific Affairs. 1996. "Health Care Needs of Gay Men and Lesbians in the United States." *Journal of the American Medical Association* 275:1354-1359.

"An Introduction to Gaycare." Retrieved June 1, 2001, from the World Wide Web. Available online: <http://www.gaycare.com>.

Atchley, Robert C. 2000. *Social Forces and Aging: An Introduction to Social Gerontology,* Ninth Edition. Belmont, CA: Wadsworth Publishing.

Austin City Connection, 2003. "Demographics—with Census 2000 Data, Maps and Analysis." Retrieved February 14, 2003, from the World Wide Web. Available online <http://www.ci.austin.tx.us/census/>.

Berg, Bruce L. 2001. *Qualitative Research Methods for the Social Sciences,* Fourth Edition. Needham Heights, MA: Allyn & Bacon.

Berger, Raymond M. 1982. "The Unseen Minority: Older Gays and Lesbians." *Social Work* 27:236-242.

_____. 1984. "Realities of Gay and Lesbian Aging." *Social Work* 29:57-62.

_____. 1996. *Gay and Gray: The Older Homosexual Man,* Second Edition. Binghamton, NY: The Haworth Press.

Black, Betty Smith, Peter V. Rabins, and Pearl S. German. 1999. "Predictors of Nursing Home Placement Among Elderly Public Housing Residents." *The Gerontologist* 39:559-568.

Black, Betty Smith, Peter V. Rabins, Pearl S. German, Marsden McGuire, and Robert Roca. 1997. "Need and Unmet Need for Mental Health Care Among Elderly Public Housing Residents." *The Gerontologist* 37:717-728.

Black, Dan, Gary Gates, Seth Sanders, and Lowell Taylor. 2000. "Demographics of the Gay and Lesbian Population in the United States: Evidence from Available Systematic Data Sources." *Demography,* 37(2): 139-154.

Blumer, Herbert. 1969. *Symbolic Interactionism: Perspective and Method.* Los Angeles: University of California Press.

Cahill, Sean, Ken South, and Jane Spade. 2000. "Outing Age: Public Policy Issues Affecting Gay, Lesbian, Bisexual, and Transgender Elders." The Policy Institute of the National Gay and Lesbian Task Force Foundation. Washington, DC.

Carlson, Helena M. and Joanne Steuer. 1985. "Age, Sex-Role Categorization, and Psychological Health in American Homosexual and Heterosexual Men and Women." *The Journal of Social Psychology* 125:203-211.

Centers for Disease Control and Prevention. 2001a. "Basic Statistics: Cumulative AIDS Cases." National Center for HIV, STD, and TB Prevention. Division of

HIV/AIDS Prevention. Retrieved May 15, 2001, from the World Wide Web. Available online: <http://www.cdc.gov/hiv/stats/cumulati.htm>.

_____. 2001b. "HIV/AIDS Surveillance Report." National Center for HIV, STD, and TB Prevention. Division of HIV/AIDS Prevention. Vol. 13, No. 2. Retrieved May 15, 2001, from the World Wide Web. Available online: <http://www. cdc. gov/hiv/stats/hasr1302.pdf>.

_____. 2001c. "HIV/AIDS Update." Retrieved from the World Wide Web. Available online: <http//www.cdc.gov/nchstp/od/news/At-a-Glance.pdf>.

City of Houston 2003. "About Houston: Houston Facts." Retrieved February 14, 2003, from the World Wide Web. Available online: <http://www.ci.houston.tx. us/abouthouston/ houstonfacts.html>.

Dallas Facts and Statistical Profile 2003. Retrieved February 14, 2003, from the World Wide Web. Available online: <http//www.dallascityhall.com/dallas/eng/ html/statistical_profile.html>.

DeCrescenzo, Teresa A. 1984. "Homophobia: A Study of the Attitudes of Mental Health Professionals Toward Homosexuality." *Homosexuality and Social Work* 2:115-136.

Devlin, Jone. 2000. "Unspoken Voices: The Graying of Gay America." *The Texas Triangle* 43:22-23.

Dorfman, Rachelle, Karina Walters, Patrick Burke, Loida Hardin, Theresa Karanik, John Raphael, and Ellen Silverstein. 1995. "Old, Sad, and Alone: The Myth of the Aging Homosexual." *Journal of Gerontological Social Work* 24:29-44.

Emlet, Charles A. 1997. "HIV/AIDS in the Elderly: A Hidden Population." *Home Care Provider* 2:69-75.

Federal Interagency Forum on Aging Related Statistics. "Older Americans 2000: Key Indicators of Well-Being." 2000. Washington, DC: U.S. Government Printing Office.

Fields, J. and Casper, L.M. 2001. "America's Families and Living Arrangements: March 2000." Current (1) Population Reports, P20-537, U.S. Census Bureau, Washington, DC.

Fokkema, Tineke, and Leo Van Wissen. 1997. "Moving Plans of the Elderly: A Test of the Stress-Threshold Model." *Environment and Planning* 29:249-268.

Fort, Joel, Claude M. Steiner, and Florence Conrad. 1971. "Attitudes of Mental Health Professionals Toward Homosexuality and Its Treatment." *Psychological Reports* 29:347-350.

Fredriksen, Karen I. 1999. "Family Caregiving Responsibilities Among Lesbians and Gay Men." *Social Work* 44:142-155.

Friend, Richard A. 1990. "Older Lesbian and Gay People: Responding to Homophobia." *Homosexuality and Family Relations* 20:241-263.

_____. 1991. "Older Lesbian and Gay People: A Theory of Successful Aging." *Journal of Homosexuality* 20:99-118.

Galassi, Frank S. 1991. "A Life-Review Workshop for Gay and Lesbian Elders." *Journal of Gerontological Social Work* 16:75-86.

Gay and Lesbian Medical Association and LGBT Health Experts. 2001. "Healthy People 2010 Companion Document for Lesbian, Gay, Bisexual, and Transgender

(LGBT) Health." Retrieved June 1, 2001, from the World Wide Web. Available online: <http://www.glma.org/policy/hp2010/PDF/HP2010CDLGBTHealth.pdf>.

Gochros, Harvey L. 1984. "Teaching Social Workers to Meet the Needs of the Homosexually Oriented." *Homosexuality and Social Work* 2:137-156.

Goffman, Erving. 1963. *Stigma: Notes on the Management of Spoiled Identity.* New York: Simon & Schuster.

Gordon, Steven M. and Sumner Thompson. 1995. "The Changing Epidemiology of Human Immunodeficiency Virus Infection in Older Persons." *Journal of the American Geriatrics Society* 43:7-9.

Gubrium, Jaber F. and James A. Holstein. 1995. "Life Course Malleability: Biographical Work and Deprivatization." *Sociological Inquiry* 65:207-223.

_____. 1998. "Narrative Practice and the Coherence of Personal Stories." *The Sociological Quarterly* 39:163-187.

_____. 1999. "At the Border of Narrative and Ethnography." *Journal of Contemporary Ethnography* 28:561-573.

Kelly, Jim. 1977. "The Aging Male Homosexual: Myth and Reality." *The Gerontologist* 17:328-332.

Kertzner, Robert. 1999. "Self-Appraisal of Life Experience and Psychological Adjustment in Midlife Gay Men." *Journal of Psychology and Human Sexuality* 11:43-64.

Kimmel, Douglas C. 1978. "Adult Development and Aging: A Gay Perspective." *Journal of Social Issues* 34:113:130.

Kowalewski, Mark R. 1988. "Double Stigma and Boundary Maintenance: How Gay Men Deal with AIDS." *Journal of Contemporary Ethnography* 17:211-228.

Kukoleck, Kevin J. (Ed.). 1999. "Housing Our Own: Snapshots of Initiatives Across the U.S." 1999. *Outword* 6(1):3-6.

Lipman, Aaron. 1986. "Homosexual Relationships: Which Factors in the Aging Process Are Different for Homosexuals Because of Their Life-Style Choices?" *Generations* 4:51-54.

Litwin, Howard. 1998. "The Provision of Information Support by Elderly People Residing in Assisted Living Facilities." *The Gerontologist* 28:239-246.

Lofland, John and Lyn H. Lofland. 1995. *Analyzing Social Settings.* Belmont, CA: Wadsworth Publishing.

Lucco, A.J. 1987. "Planned Retirement Housing Preferences of Older Homosexuals." *Journal of Homosexuality* 14(3/4):35-56.

Markham, John P. and John I. Gilderbloom. 1998. "Housing Quality Among the Elderly: A Decade of Changes." *International Journal of Aging and Human Development* 46:71-90.

McDonald, Jerry W. 1998. "An Analysis of the Service and Housing Needs of Gay Senior Males." Problem in lieu of thesis, University of North Texas.

McDougall, Graham J. 1993. "Therapeutic Issues with Gay and Lesbian Elders." *Clinical Gerontologist* 14:45-57.

Meyer, Julie. 2000. "Age: 2000. Census 2000 Brief." Washington, DC: U.S. Census Bureau.

Minnigerode, Fred A. and Marcy R. Adelman. 1978. "Elderly Homosexual Women and Men: Report on a Pilot Study." *Family Coordinator* 27:451-456.

Moody, Harry R. 1998. *Aging: Concepts and Controversies.* Thousand Oaks, CA: Pine Forge Press.

Moss, Robert J. and Steven H. Miles. 1987. "AIDS and the Geriatrician." *Journal of the American Geriatric Society* 35:460-464.

Office of Disease Prevention and Health Promotion, U.S. Department of Health and Human Services. 2001a. "Healthy People 2010: Healthy People in Healthy Communities." Retrieved May 12, 2001, from the World Wide Web. Available online: <http://www.healthypeople.gov>.

_____. 2001b. "Healthy People: What Are Its Goals?" Retrieved May 12, 2001, from the World Wide Web. Available online: <http://www.healthypeople.gov/About/goals.htm>

Original Prime Timers Worldwide. 2000. Retrieved September 28, 2000, from the World Wide Web. Available online: <http://www.primetimers.www.org/AboutPTW. html>.

Page, Stewart. 1998. "Accepting the Gay Person: Rental Accomodation in the Community." *Journal of Homosexuality* 36:31-39.

Papalia, Diane E., Cameron J. Camp, and Ruth Duskin Feldman. 1996. *Adult Development and Aging.* New York: McGraw Hill.

Rosenfeld, Dana. 1999. "Identity Work Among Lesbian and Gay Elderly." *Journal of Aging Studies* 13:121-144.

Ross, Michael W., James A. Paulsen, and Olli W. Stalstrom. 1988. "Homosexuality and Mental Health: A Cross-Cultural Review." *Journal of Homosexuality* 15:131-152.

Rowe, John W. and Robert L. Kahn. 1997. "Successful Aging." *The Gerontologist* 37:433-440.

San Antonio, Texas. 2003. Retrieved February 15, 2003, from The World Wide Web. Available online:<http://www.factmonster.com/ipka/A0108587.html>.

Scharnhorst, Susanne. 1992. "AIDS Dementia Complex in the Elderly: Diagnosis and Management." *Nurse Practitioner: A Journal of Primary Health Care* 17:37,41-43.

Slusher, Morgan P., Carole J. Mayer, and Ruth E. Dunkle. 1996. "Gays and Lesbians Older and Wiser (GLOW): A Support Group for Older Gay People." *The Gerontologist* 36:118-123.

Smith, Denise and Hava Tillipman. 2000. "The Older Population in the United States: Population Characteristics." Washington, DC: U.S. Census Bureau.

Spradley, James P. 1979. *The Ethnographic Interview.* New York: Holt, Rinehart, and Winston.

_____. 1980. *Participant Observation.* New York: Holt, Rinehart, and Winston.

Stephens, Dale E. and Carl "Lucky" Wheat. 2001. "Gay San Antonio." 2001. Retrieved January 10, 2001, from the World Wide Web. Available online: <http://www.gay-sa.com/mission.htm>.

Templer, Donald I., Dave Velber, Miriam Lovito, John A. Testa, and Chris Knippers. 1983. "The Death Anxiety of Gays." *Omega* 14:211-214.

Thompson, Estina E. and Neal Krause. 1998. "Living Alone and Neighborhood Characteristics As Predictors of Social Support in Late Life." *Journal of Gerontology* 53:354-364.

Thompson, George H. and William R. Fishburn. 1977. "Attitudes Toward Homosexuality Among Graduate Counseling Students." *Counselor Education and Supervision* 17:121-130.

U.S. Census Bureau. 2000. "Projections of the Total Resident Population by 5-Year Age Groups and Sex with Special Age Categories: Middle Series, 2025 to 2045." (NP-T3-F). Population Projections Program, Population Division, U.S. Census Bureau. Released January 13, 2000.

_____. 2003. "Projections of the Population, by Age and Sex, of States: 1995 to 2025." Retrieved February 15, 2003, from the World Wide Web. Available online: <http:/www.census.gov/population/projections/state/stpjage.txt.>.

Wallace, Jeffrey I., Douglas S. Paauw, and David H. Spach. 1993. "HIV Infection in Older Patients: When to Expect the Unexpected." *Geriatrics* 48:61-70.

Woodman, Natalie J. 1989. "Mental Health Issues of Relevance to Lesbian Women and Gay Men." *Journal of Gay and Lesbian Psychotherapy* 1:53-63.

Index

Page numbers followed by the letter "t" indicate tables.